Things You Can Do To Defend Your Gun Rights

Other Books by the Authors

By Alan M. Gottlieb

The Rights of Gun Owners

The Gun Grabbers

Gun Rights Fact Book

By David B. Kopel

The Samurai, the Mountie, and Cowboy: Should America Adopt the Gun Controls of Other Democracies?

Gun Control in Great Britain: Saving Lives or Constricting Liberty?

Things You Can Do To Defend Your Gun Rights

By

Alan Gottlieb

and

Dave Kopel

MERRIL PRESS
BELLEVUE, WASHINGTON

Things You Can Do To Defend Your Gun Rights

A Merril Press Book
published by arrangement with the authors

For information, permissions, or additional copies of this book, contact Merril Press, P.O. Box 1682, Bellevue, Washington 98009. Telephone (206) 454-7009

$9.95   ISBN: 0-936783-10-9

Printed in the United States of America

Table of Contents

Dedication

To our wives Deirdre and Julie, our best friends.

User's Warning

This book attempts to provide information about methods to preserve and protect the rights we all share. Some of the advice is based on first-hand experience, and some is based on recommendations of others. While we've tried to make the book as accurate as possible, we can't promise or guarantee particular results. It is the reader's responsibility to put the book to use in an appropriate manner.

A Note on Usage

Half the people in country are female, so we thought it inappropriate to use "he" and "him" exclusively. At the same time, we thought it cumbersome to always say "he or she." So some of the time we use "he" by itself, and sometimes we use "she" by itself. The gender pronoun chosen never has any significance, and everything in this book applies equally to men and women.

Introduction

"IF JUST ONE TENTH OF THE PEOPLE IN THIS COUNTRY
WHO OWN GUNS WOULD RAISE THEIR VOICES TO THE
POLITICIANS, OR CONTRIBUTE A SMALL AMOUNT OF
THEIR TIME AND MONEY, WE COULD STOP THE BAN-
THE-GUN CROWD."
                        —Former California State Assemblyman
                                               Tom McClintock

If you own a gun, you can defend yourself against a criminal attack. But how can you defend yourself against people who want to take away your right to even own a gun? This book tells you how.

In the struggle over the right to bear arms, the gun prohibitionists start with a tremendous organizational advantage. The anti-gun movement is hierarchical—that is, its direction comes from the top down. A few professional strategists decide the issue of the year: how a waiting period will supposedly stop drug dealers from getting guns (how about a waiting period for drugs, so they couldn't get drugs either); how "plastic handguns" are being used by terrorists (even though there's no such thing as a plastic handgun); the record numbers of toddlers being killed in gun accidents (record low, that is); the epidemic of mass murder by "assault weapon" (another gun control fib).

From there, the gun control lobbies feed the story to their ventriloquist dummies in the media, such as Dan Rather and Tom Brokaw. The establishment media's contempt for gun owners is so intense that the veracity of the story is of little import. Thus, a new issue is born. Politicians who confuse media opinion with public opinion are intimidated into enacting more and more severe restrictions on gun owners.

The right to bear arms movement, in contrast, works from the grassroots up. We don't get hundred of millions of dollars in free advertising (thinly disguised as news shows) from the media. The strength of the right to bear arms movement comes almost entirely from individual citizens who take up the burden of defending the rights of all Americans. Thus, the battle is joined: the prohibition forces and the media, versus ordinary citizens.

Happily, ordinary citizens can do some things in large numbers that Dan Rather can't: they can write letters to Congress; they can vote gun prohibitionists out of office; and they can even push the media to re-examine its attitudes. We can pass on a free society to the next generations—if we will roll up our sleeves to do the hard work of preserving liberty.

Of course there are plenty of excuses for not getting involved, like:

● *The NRA will take care of everything.* The problem is that the power of the NRA, and the rest of the pro-rights movement, is based on grassroots strength.

● *Other people don't do their share, so why should I?* Well, lots of other people, including the folks we mention in this book, do their share and a whole lot more.

● *The gun confiscators are going to win no matter what we do.* The gun control lobbies certainly want you to think that. But they're wrong. In the last 20 years, America has become significantly more urbanized. Yet in many states, the right to bear arms is stronger than it was 20 years ago.

The name of this book *isn't* "The 500 Commandments." You don't have to do everything suggested here; and unless you have 48 hours in a day, you couldn't anyway. While some of the ideas are very simple to implement (e.g., register to vote, join the NRA), many others take a lot of follow-through. For the more time-consuming projects, take on just one or two at a time, starting with the ones that best fit your inclinations and talents. As you gain experience in the struggle for freedom, new ideas and projects will suggest themselves.

While these ideas are geared towards Second Amendment issues, many of our suggestions are just as applicable to folks who are fighting to protect other freedoms in the Bill of Rights. We hope this book is useful to them as well.

PART I

EDUCATING YOURSELF — AND OTHERS

American writer Gertrude Stein once described her hometown Oakland: "When you get there, there isn't any there there." Gun control is a lot like Oakland: There isn't any reality there. The people who want to take your guns have loads of misplaced emotion, prejudice, and disinformation to feed the press. But they're in short supply of facts and statistics.

This section details the public information side of the gun rights debate: how to inform yourself about the issues, and how to inform others.

1. Feed Your Head: Books

"THE THINGS I WANT TO KNOW ARE IN BOOKS; MY
BEST FRIEND IS THE MAN WHO'LL GET ME A BOOK I
AIN'T READ."   —Abraham Lincoln

Defenders of the right to bear arms have facts and logic on their side, but the gun prohibitionists have the media on their side. Most people get their information only from the media; hence, most people are badly misinformed about the facts of the gun issue. One of the responsibilities of being a gun owner is rationally explaining the facts about gun ownership to your friends and acquaintances. Below is a list of some of the best books and other materials written about the right to bear arms, so you can arm yourself with knowledge.

If you're fairly new to the gun issue, the volume of materials available may seem daunting. Don't worry. There are good books for every level of knowledge about the right to bear arms.

Starters

Research Reports published by the Second Amendment Foundation are a series of short and informative pamphlets about various aspects of the right to keep and bear arms. The Reports are issued as the result of SAF's continuous research into the social, political, and legal aspects of firearm rights. Current titles include: *Supreme Court Decisions Regarding The Second Amendment*; *Saving Seven Days Time While Fighting Crime: Instant Background Checks as an Alternative to the Brady Bill*; *The Role of Firearms In Self Defense*; *Bans on Semi-Automatics: Unconstitutional Hysteria*; *Handgun Control: Its Threat to Rifle & Shotgun Ownership*; *Handgun Purchase Waiting Periods: Do they Reduce Crime?* Each of these reports are fact-filled sources for knowledge about gun use and ownership in America.

The reports are available at no charge from the Second Amendment Foundation, 12500 NE 10th Place, Bellevue, WA 98005 1-206-454-7012.

The National Rifle Association's Institute for Legislative Action (NRA/ILA) publishes its own set of short brochures about gun control issues. Titles include: *Ten Myths About Gun Control, Gun Law Failures, A Push for Gun Control, Criminals Don't Wait—Why Should You?, Semi-Automatic Firearms: A Citizen's Choice, The Armed Citizen, Don't Buy HCI Lies, 1993 NRA Firearms Fact Card, It Can Happen to You, Interstate Transportation,* and *1993 Compendium of State Laws.* NRA also publishes short brochures about the gun laws of each state, as well as separate brochures for Washington, DC and New York City (two jurisdictions whose low crime rates prove how effective gun control really is.) The booklets can be obtained from Information and Member Services, NRA/ILA. For the NRA's address and telephone, see chapter 25.

Books: Two Basics

The material in the SAF Research Reports and in the NRA/ILA brochures is a good starting point for educating yourself on the gun issue. If you don't have much time for reading, the Reports and brochures provide you with well-researched quick summaries of issues. But as a Second Amendment activist, you'll likely be interested in learning more and more about the issue, for your own interest, as well as to provide support for your activist work.

An excellent first book on the gun issue *The Rights of Gun Owners* by Alan Gottlieb. This compilation of all federal and state laws relating to guns and ammunition includes everything from constitutional guarantees to licenses, regulations, concealed weapons, waiting periods, ammunition purchases, postal regulations, and crossing state borders. This book details what your rights are, how those rights are being destroyed, and how to protect yourself from a government grown too powerful. For those concerned about the preservation and extension of freedom of gun ownership, this book is a very good primer.

$9.95 from Merril Press, P.O. Box 1682, Bellevue, WA 98009. To order by phone call 1-206-454-7009.

Another fine first book (and a good second book as well) is the *Gun Rights Fact Book*, also by Alan Gottlieb. The book is easy to read, and organized by topic (i.e., "Media Bias", "Plastic Guns"). The book is an excellent source for key facts about just about every gun control issue.

The book is not footnoted, so it's not particularly suited as a starting point for research on gun control.

If you're already a gun rights activist, you may already know much of the information presented in the *Gun Rights Fact Book.* If so, the book is a good tool for you to use by giving it to your less-informed pro-gun friends.

$9.95 from the Merril Press, P.O. Box 1682, Bellevue, WA 98009, same phone number as above.

Just the Facts, Ma'am

Once you're ready to plunge in a little deeper, there are several sources that provide good overall coverage of the gun control issue in a readable format. These sources, while written in an accessible style, are aimed at a somewhat more sophisticated audience than the two Alan Gottlieb books we just described. These sources also contain extensive footnotes or endnotes which, while not providing an obstacle to persons who just want to read the main text, allow persons who want to press deeper to find out where to go.

Guns, Murders, and the Constitution: A Realistic Assessment of Gun Control is a gem by Don B. Kates, Jr. For the last two decades, Kates has been the star intellectual of the pro-gun movement. Kates' prodigious writing has been published in popular magazines like *Harpers* and scholarly journals like the *Michigan Law Review* that had never before printed anything pro-gun. Virtually every academic who has defended the right to bear arms has consulted with Kates. A prolific pro-Second Amendment writer, Kates has opened up more minds on the subject of gun control than anyone in the history of the United States. This 64 page velo-bound monograph (short study) is an excellent summary Kates' work, particularly regarding the evidence about gun control and self-defense.

Kates demolishes the myth that domestic homicides are perpetrated by nice people who just happened to have a gun around when their wife burned the dinner, dissects the pompous assertions of white male academics that women are better off submitting to rape than resisting with a gun, and puts to rest the anti-gun lobby's phony claims about childhood gun accidents. Eight dollars from the Pacific Research Institute for Public Policy, 177 Post St., San Francisco, CA 94108. 1-415-989-0833.

Trust the People: The Case Against Gun Control, by David B. Kopel. Here's a review from gun activist Neal Knox's computer bulletin board: "A relatively short (32 typewritten pages) well documented (plus 20 pages of references) overview of the basic issues. One of the best things you can use to convince an individual with a potentially open mind. It's fact filled, well written, forcefully argued, and makes sure to hit all the right liberal hot buttons (civil rights, racial and sexual discrimination, etc.). For the price, you have no excuse for not getting it."

$4 from the Cato Institute, 1000 Mass. Ave. NW, Washington DC 20001-5403. (202) 842-0200. Request "Policy Analysis #109, Trust the People."

The Gun Control Debate: You Decide, by Lee Nisbet provides an excellent pro-and-con overview of the gun control topic. Nisbet went to pro-rights and pro-control organizations, and asked them to suggest the best essays which had been written in favor of their respective positions. The 24 essays collected in Nisbet's book offer a "greatest hits" collection of pro-rights scholarship, and also provide an up-close look at the best material the pro-control side has to offer. The contrast in the quality of scholarship between the pro-rights side and the pro-control side is sometimes startling. Studying the pro-control essays gives you a heads-up on the arguments you will most likely encounter from pro-control folks.

Available from Prometheus Books, Buffalo, NY, 800-767-1241 (24 hours), or from Merril Press (address and phone above).

Advanced Stuff

Without any doubt, one book stands out at the single best source of information about guns and gun control in America: *Point Blank: Guns and Violence in America*, by Gary Kleck. Simply put, *Point Blank* is the best overview of gun control that can be found. Summarizing the findings of other scholars, and presenting original research, Kleck demonstrates the folly of harsh gun controls.

Is the average gun owner so stupid and clumsy that he risks killing himself accidentally with the gun he brought for protection? Kleck analyzes gun accidents in detail, and shows that most accident perpetrators are outrageously reckless and irresponsible, and have little in common with the average gun owner. Kleck also observes that most "accidents" said to occur while cleaning a gun are really suicides.

Is the gun in the home or business a menace to society? Just the opposite. Through thoroughly documented numerical data, Kleck shows that Americans use handguns at least 645,000 times a year for self-defense (usually without needing to fire a shot). The high rate of American gun ownership explains why burglary of occupied residences is so low in comparison to the rates in other countries. Overall, an American criminal's chances of getting shot by his victim are at least as great as his chances of going to jail.

Have gun registration, gun prohibition, or any of the rest of the gun control litany had any statistically perceptible effect in reducing crime? The answer is "no," suggests Kleck, and he does a particularly good job in skewering the pseudo-science that the anti-gun lobbies claim supports their cause.

While intended to be accessible to a general readership, *Point Blank* is written for a rigorous academic audience. Accordingly, some paragraphs of the book delve into technical discussion of quantitative sociology that will be over the head of anyone without at least two semesters of a college statistics classes and a fond memory of slide rules.

The book is well-organized, with a strong table of contents, index, subheadings, and other reader aids. Thus, instead of reading the book straight through, you can use it as a guide to all the research regarding gun control in modern America. So when you want to write a letter to the editor and supply the real facts about the (extremely low) rate of childhood gun accidents, *Point Blank* will have all the information available right there. And every chapter is supplemented by at least a half-dozen tables providing a wealth of statistics about guns and their use.

In short, *Point Blank* is a book that deserves to be read by anyone with a serious interest in the gun control debate. Scrupulously honest, Kleck comes to the politically incorrect conclusion that guns save lives, and gun control does not. As a result, Kleck has been vilified by anti-gun forces such as *The New Republic* magazine, in thoughtless editorials that attack Kleck by misstating what he says.

While coming under fire from the anti-gun forces, *Point Blank* is not entirely supportive of the pro-gun side. In the rare cases where the evidence shows that a particular gun control has worked, Kleck says so.

And while Kleck demonstrates the useless or dangerous nature of most of the gun control lobby's agenda, Kleck does propose his own set of controls.

Kleck favors a national "instant check" on all gun sales. He would require that even transfers between private individuals be routed through licensed gun dealers, so that the instant check could be applied to those transactions.

About 84% of gun sales could be approved immediately, as with a credit card check. But for the other sales, Kleck admits, a substantial number of legitimate buyers would be disapproved initially, and then required to go through a weekslong process to clear their names, thanks to the poor quality of criminal justice records in many states. (For example, if you have the same name as someone who was arrested for a nonviolent felony, and was later found not guilty, you could easily be turned down by the "instant check.")

Moreover, background checks of any kind, including the "instant check" do sometimes find ineligible buyers, but almost never catch a criminal trying to acquire a crime gun. The typical "criminal" caught by a background check is more like the man who got into a fist fight in a bar ten years ago, and never realized that his third-degree assault conviction disqualified him from owning a gun.

And besides, the very rare criminal who can't get a black market gun, and who wants to buy a crime gun from a gun store, can simply ask a friend with a clean record to make the purchase for him.

The negligible benefits of the instant check are outweighed by their substantial costs, which Kleck fails to fully consider. First of all, a large new government bureaucracy would be required to administer the check. Kleck suggests paying for the bureaucracy through a $10/gun purchase. While ten dollars may not seem like much to a hunter buying a $500 rifle, it's quite a bit to a young woman who can barely afford $40 for a self-defense handgun. Moreover, once the tax was established, the anti-gun lobbies would immediately begin pressing to raise it as high as possible.

Like almost every scholar who has studied the issue, Kleck agrees that the Second Amendment guarantees an individual right to bear arms. Yet the Kleck instant check amounts to people being restrained from exercising their Constitutional rights until the government gives them permission. Kleck, who is a strong civil libertarian, ought to be more sensitive to the Constitutional policy against prior restraints.

And lastly, it's very difficult to design an instant check system that can't be perverted into a registry of gun owners.

But whatever you think of Kleck's conclusions, his book on the whole is outstanding. It is precisely the kind of carefully argued, meticulously researched scholarship that the gun debate needs. If you ever speak out regarding the right to bear arms, if you ever write letters to the editor, if you ever write your state legislators, you will find *Point Blank* a wonderful resource.

Point Blank is published by Aldine de Gruyter (Hawthorne, New York), and is available in high-quality bookstores. Any bookstore can special order it for you.

Unfortunately, *Point Blank*, is published only in hard cover, and at 512 pages, the book retails for a very hefty $59.95.

Despite the high price, *Point Blank* is worth every penny. If you can't afford it, ask your local library to buy it. Most libraries that get two or three requests for a book within a few weeks will strongly consider a purchase.

Under the Gun: Weapons Crime & Violence, by James Wright, Peter Rossi, and Kathleen Daly. The authors are some of the best sociologists in the United States. They favored gun control, and set out to collect all the evidence for it in one place. This book is the result. After taking a hard look at the data, the authors changed their minds, and announced that there is no proof that gun control does any good. The book's only serious limitation is that it was written in the early 1980s, and therefore does not cover some of the more recent research, and does not discuss some of the issues that have arisen in recent years, such as so-called "assault weapons."

$44.95 cloth, $24.95 paperback from Aldine de Gruyter, 200 Saw Mill River Rd., Hawthorne, NY 10532. 1-914-747-0110.

Armed and Dangerous, by Jim Wright and Peter Rossi reports the results of a 1981 National Institute of Justice study of felony prisoners in ten state prison systems. The study provides overwhelming evidence of how guns in the right hands enhance public safety: 56% percent of the prisoners said that a criminal would not attack a potential victim who was known to be armed. Thirty-nine percent of the felons had personally decided not to commit a crime because they thought the victim might have a gun, and 8% said the experience had occurred "many times." Criminals in states with higher civilian gun ownership rates worried the most about armed victims. At the same time, the criminals reported that gun control laws had little or no effect on their ability to obtain crime guns.

Like *Under the Gun,* the book is published by Aldine de Gruyter, 200 Saw Mill River Rd., Hawthorne, NY 10532. 1-914-747-0110. Prices are $39.95 cloth, and $19.95 paperback.

The *Journal on Firearms and Public Policy*. Published by the Center for the Study of Firearms & Public Policy, the *Journal* provides a forum for publication of scholarly articles on firearms and their relation to social, legal, and political issues. It accepts papers on a broad range of scholarly topics related to gun ownership, use, carrying, law and policy issues. The *Journal* also reprints important past articles in order to provide a unified reference source for researching firearms issues.

The primary purposes of the *Journal* are to encourage serious researchers to explore issues related to firearms and their effect on society; to provide a convenient place for the publication of research results; and to provide an information source which can be used by policy makers to guide their decisions. The Second Amendment Foundation sponsors the *Journal* to encourage objective research. It is the intention of the editors to reprint articles of scholarly quality regardless of their conclusions for or against the Foundation's positions on controversial issues.

Volumes 1 and 2 are nearly out of print and available in limited quantities only. Volumes 3 and 4 will likely remain available for the next few years. Volume 3 includes a reprint of University of Texas Law Professor Sanford Levinson's groundbreaking essay on the Second Amendment; an article on law-enforcement lobbying and the Second Amendment, by NRA researcher Paul Blackman; a short article on how gun control endangers all Constitutional rights, by attorney David I. Caplan; and an original article "Gun-making as a Cottage Industry," which discusses the types of handguns that would be produced by home workshops in the event of gun prohibition.

Volume 4 includes an article analyzing New York City's law requiring mandatory jail terms for illegal gun possession; several articles about the original meaning of the Second Amendment; and an article about the unintended consequences of gun control.

Issues available, for ten dollars apiece, from the Second Amendment Foundation, 12500 NE 10th Place, Bellevue, WA 98005 1-206-454-7012.

Law Abiding Criminals by John Kaplan, Don Kates, and Raymond Kessler. The purpose of this monograph, which contains three articles by noted sociologists and criminologists, is to illustrate the lesson learned time and again that government is not an effective instrument for social engineering. That is, history has proven that when government outlaws something desired by a substantial segment of a population, the populace simply ignores the government edict or devises methods to circumvent the law. Ultimately, once the law is recognized as a failure, it is abandoned, but in the meantime what has been accomplished is to make otherwise law-abiding Americans members of the criminal class.

Law-Abiding Criminals was produced to present the views of those who question the efficacy of an all-encompassing handgun ban. Written by individuals with first-hand experience in the criminal-defense field, the authors share a common opinion that a total handgun ban would experience enforcement difficulties similar to those encountered during alcohol prohibition and drug interdiction campaigns.

Available from the Second Amendment Foundation, 1250 NE 10th Place, Bellevue, WA 98005. 1-206-454-7012.

History of the Right to Bear Arms

That Every Man Be Armed: The Evolution of a Constitutional Right, by Stephen P. Halbrook: This is by far the best historical book of the legal development of the Second Amendment in the United States. The research is thorough, and the reasoning insightful. The book has been accorded the high honor of being cited as an authoritative source in an article in the *Yale Law Journal*—Akhil Reed Amar's "The Bill of Rights as a Constitution," (vol. 100). Liberty Tree Press, 1-800-345-2888; $12.95.

Halbrook's other book, *A Right to Bear Arms: State and Federal Bills of Rights and Constitutional Guarantees* is less essential. The book is mostly a history of state arms right guarantees in the during the American Revolution and Early Republic. For a historian, the book is an indispensable reference. For a general reader, it may be too densely written. The very steep price slapped on the book by publisher *Greenwood Press* is an indication that the market is library sales more than the average gun owner. Greenwood Press, 88 Post Road West, Westport, CT 06881.

The Right to Keep and Bear Arms, Report of the US Senate Subcommittee on the Constitution. In 1982, the US Senate decided to take a look at the original intent of the authors of the Second Amendment. The Senate Subcommittee on the Constitution *unanimously* concluded that the Second Amendment guarantees an individual right to keep and bear arms. Although the Government Printing Office version of the book has gone out of print, the book has been reprinted by the Second Amendment Foundation. 1-206-454-7012. The book is also reprinted volume 1 of *Gun Control and the Constitution* (discussed below).

The Origin of the Second Amendment, by David Young. The book reprints 480 documents from the period surrounding the introduction and ratification of the Second Amendment. Included are newspaper articles, pamphlets, letters to the editor, debates from the federal Constitutional convention, debates from the state ratifying conventions, and Congressional debates.

Author David Young has brought together, for the first time, all of the original source material regarding what the Second Amendment meant to the nation that enacted it. The book opens in the summer of 1787 with the federal Constitutional Convention debating Congressional powers regarding the militia.

The final major document of the book is a January 29, 1791 article in the *Independent Gazetteer* (a Philadelphia newspaper), in which the author, who identifies himself only as "A Farmer" warns: "Under every government the dernier [last] resort of the people, is an appeal to the sword; whether to defend themselves against the open attacks of a foreign enemy, or to check the insidious encroachments of domestic foes."

In between the first and last documents is a treasure-trove of American history. Leafing through these pages, you encounter the great men who founded our Republic, and whose words speak to us today. Wrote Tench Coxe, James Madison's friend, in the Feb. 20, 1778 *Freeman's Journal*: "Who are the militia? *are they not our selves*...Their swords, and ever other terrible implement of the soldier, are *the birthright of an American*." (emphasis in original.)

Hear Patrick Henry thundering from the June 5, 1788 Virginia ratifying convention: "Guard with jealous attention the public liberty. Suspect every one who approaches that jewel. Unfortunately, nothing will preserve it but downright force. Whenever you give up that force you are inevitably ruined."

The men who speak to us through *The Origin of the Second Amendment* harbor no fear that government would interfere with "sporting" guns or hunting. They express the greatest apprehension of select, uniformed military forces, such as the standing army (and such as the modern National Guard).

As *The Origin of the Second Amendment* makes unmistakably clear, the great object of the Second Amendment was to preserve liberty by ensuring that the American people would have in their individual hands the weapons with which to resist federal tyranny. The "well-regulated militia" included almost every able-bodied free male.

Besides collecting an excellent selection of documents, the author also provides a good introductory essay summarizing the historical context of the debate over ratification of the Constitution and the Bill of Rights, as well as an appendix giving the full text of all state Bill of Rights from 1787-89, and a very detailed index. This book was awarded the "Book of the Year" prize by *Gun World* magazine in 1992.

The Origin of the Second Amendment is available by mail from Golden Oak Books, 605 Michigan Street, Ontonagon, Michigan 49953, or can be special-ordered by your local bookstore (supply them with the Michigan address, since the publisher is not well-known). The book goes for $50 plus $5 shipping and handling (plus 4% sales tax for Michigan residents).

Origins and Developments of the Second Amendment, by David Hardy. In 95 very readable pages, Hardy traces the right to bear arms from its origins in early English history up through the creation of the American Second Amendment. The book is broken down into subtopics, about one per page. Each subtopic contains a two or three paragraph quote from an original source (such as an English King's law), coupled with analysis from Hardy.

The result? A straightforward history of the history of our right to bear arms, that serves as an excellent introduction to the topic.

At the same time, the book's long quotations from original sources are very useful for more advanced students of the right to bear arms.

Hardy's fine book can be special ordered from your local bookstore. Or you can order the book directly from the publisher, Blacksmith Corp., at 1-800-531-2665.

Specialized Topics

The Gun Culture and Its Enemies, edited by William R. Tonso, takes a detailed look at some neglected angles of the gun control debate.

The book includes chapters by sociologist William Tonso and by Kopel demonstrating the existence of media bias in coverage of gun control. In another chapter, John Salter, a veteran of the civil rights movement, details how the use of armed force by civil rights workers in the 1960s was crucial to the movement's success—because it deterred murders by the Ku Klux Klan.

Do sexually inadequate people buy guns to serve as substitute phallic symbols? Don Kates and Nicole Varzos demolish the notion in their chapter.

The Gun Culture and Its Enemies can be ordered for $9.95 in paperback from Merril Press, P.O. Box 1682, Bellevue, Washington, 98009. 1-206-454-7009.

The Samurai, the Mountie, and the Cowboy: Should America Adopt the Gun Controls of Other Democracies?, by

David B. Kopel. Everyone has heard the argument: Other countries have gun control; other countries have less gun crime, so if we had strict gun control, we'd have less gun crime. In a comprehensive analysis, *The Samurai* debunks the myth that gun control is responsible for the low crime rates in Japan, Britain, Canada, and other democracies. The book also offers a provocative survey of the history of firearms, violence, and crime in America.

Best-selling novelist Tom Clancy praised the book as "A superb piece of scholarship, admirable for its integrity and painstaking research. Kopel provides the fresh air of reason in a national debate too often marked by acrimony and prejudice." The book was awarded the Comparative Criminology Book Award by the American Society of Criminology's Division of Comparative and International Criminology.

$28.95 plus shipping, available from the Second Amendment Foundation, 1250 NE 10th Place, Bellevue, WA 98005. 1-206-454-7012. Also available from the publisher, Prometheus Books, at 1-800-767-1241 (24 hours).

Why Gun Waiting Periods Threaten Public Safety, by David B. Kopel. The most detailed analysis available of the arguments for and against waiting periods. 62 pages, stapled.

$8 a copy. Independence Institute, 14142 Denver West Parkway #101; Golden, CO 80401. (303) 279-6536.

The "Assault Weapon" Panic: Political Correctness Takes Aim at the Constitution, by Eric Morgan and David B. Kopel (revised edition, April 1993). A 94 page Issue Paper debunking the claims of persons who want to prohibit semiautomatics.

$12 a copy. Independence Institute, 14142 Denver West Parkway #101; Golden, CO 80401. (303) 279-6536.

Armed and Female. Author Paxton Quigley, a former anti-gun activist, explains why she now supports a woman's right to keep and bear arms. The book contains lots of practical advice for a woman considering buying a gun.

Available from the Second Amendment Foundation, 1250 NE 10th Place, Bellevue, WA 98005. 1-206-454-7012.

Gun Control: The Continuing Debate by Dr. Donald Hook. Dr. Hook, a former agent with the Federal Bureau of Investigation, is a professor at Trinity College in Hartford, Connecticut. He was educated at five US universities and OSI/FBI School in Washington DC and the Criminological Institute at the University of Vienna. He received a PhD from Brown University.

Gun Control: The Continuing Debate was written to inform the public at large, and it ought to have a place in public and academic libraries. It is an informative look at the history, sociology and governmental aspects of the gun control debate written to the high school and college level. Dr. Hook covers the field of the gun control landscape in chapters dealing with the history of the right to keep and bear arms and in chapters arguing for and against the status quo. Probably the most controversial statements made in the book occur in the final chapter where Dr. Hook outlines some compromise positions he sees as valuable.

Available from Merril Press, P.O. Box 1682, Bellevue, WA 98009, or 1-206-454-7008.

Gun Control and the Constitution. This three-volume set, edited by Rutgers University Law Professor Robert J. Cottrol is the best compilation of all viewpoints of the legal debate regarding the right to keep and bear arms. The hardcover books, brought out by Garland Publishing (New York) reprint the best judicial and scholarly analysis of the Second Amendment. For any researcher concerned with in-depth legal analysis, the books very useful.

Unfortunately, the books are also very expensive. And if you know how to use a law library, you find most of the books' material in their original sources, and read them in the library for free. On the other hand, if you can afford them, each volume will add greatly to your understanding of the legal background to the gun control debate.

Volume 1, *Sources and Explorations of the Second*

Amendment ($57.00) includes a good introductory essay by Cottrol, reprints of the US Supreme Court's three major cases dealing with the Second Amendment, six state court cases, and (perhaps best of all) a full reprint of the US Senate's 130 page investigation of the historical record about the Second Amendment., *The Right to Keep and Bear Arms* (discussed above). Significantly, the reprint includes several well-written legal reports which were attached to the Senate report in the appendix. In contrast, the Second Amendment Foundation reprint of *The Right to Keep* includes only the Senate report itself. Garland Publishing, Inc., 717 Fifth Ave., Suite 2500, NY, NY 10022. (212) 751-7447. fax (212) 308-9399.

Volume 2, *Advocates and Scholars: The Modern Debate on Gun Control* ($62.00) reprints 15 major law journal articles analyzing the Second Amendment. The selections are scrupulously balanced between pro-rights and anti-rights articles. The effect, however, is to strengthen the pro-rights position, since the pro-rights articles are so much better researched and persuasive.

Volume 3, *Special Topics on Gun Control* ($54.00) reprints 9 more law journal articles, involving specialized topics in the Second Amendment debate. Most of the articles deal with the English origins of the right to keep and bear arms, or with the connection between gun-owning and responsible citizenship, as seen by the generation that created the Second Amendment. The most interesting article, however, is final one, written by Robert Cottrol and Raymond T. Diamond, which explores the history of gun control in the United States as a method of controlling Afro-Americans.

And, if the three volume set's $173.00 price tag makes your wallet tremble with fear, there are plans to bring out a one-volume paperback (priced around $20.00) containing the best material from the three volumes. Call the publisher, at the number listed above, for availability.

Gun Control: Gateway to Tyranny. The militant pro-rights organization Jews for the Preservation of Firearms Ownership has published this interesting analysis of German gun control laws in the Nazi and pre-Nazi eras. The authors document how laws which might appear reasonable on paper were used to disarm Jews and other groups as a first step towards genocide.

$19.95 plus $2.90 shipping from JPFO, Inc., 2872 S. Wentworth Ave., Milwaukee, WI 53207. 1-414-769-0760.

Further reading

All of the above books have bibliographies which will lead you to excellent articles in scholarly journals and in magazines such as the *American Rifleman*. The material we've listed here is just a starting point. There are many other worthwhile books on the subject.

2. Spread the Word—Libraries and Other Public Reading Areas

"ENLIGHTEN THE PEOPLE GENERALLY, AND TYR-
ANNY AND OPPRESSIONS OF BODY AND MIND WILL
VANISH LIKE EVIL SPIRITS AT THE DAWN OF DAY."
—Thomas Jefferson, letter to Du Pont de
Nemours, April 24, 1816.

As you've begun to educate yourself, you can begin to educate other folks. One of the easiest ways is to get pro-rights books into your local library.

One good approach for a lone activist or a small group is to "adopt a library" and focus energy on getting pro-rights materials into that one venue. The library doesn't have to be the biggest branch in the area. In fact, the smaller libraries may be more grateful for your help.

The books you help supply may be the *only* pro-gun books in that library. When students and other persons go to the library to research the gun issue, they'll find the carefully reasoned material that you laid out for them. One book placed in one library may, over time, enlighten dozens of students (and future voters) about the realities of the right to bear arms.

At the simplest level, you can simply buy pro-rights books, and give them to the library. Librarians strongly prefer hardback books, since they stand up so much better under heavy use. Before putting down the money to buy the books for a donation, check with the librarian to make sure that the library would be interested in the book. Libraries may accept some of the books, and reject others. School libraries will probably want to review all of the offered books, to make sure that they are suitable for the relevant age group.

Of the books discussed in the previous chapter, the ones most likely to be accepted by libraries would be the hard cover editions of: *The Rights of Gun Owners*; *The Gun Control Debate*; *Pointblank*; *Under the Gun*; *Armed and Dangerous*; *That Every Man Be Armed*; *Origins of the Second Amendment*;

Origins and Development of the Second Amendment; *The Samurai, the Mountie, and the Cowboy*; *Gun Control and the Constitution*; and *Armed and Female*.

Donations can also be done on a larger scale. The People's Rights Organization, of Columbus, Ohio, working with the national Citizen's Committee for the Right to Keep and Bear Arms, bought 25 copies each of three pro-gun books and donated them to the Columbus Library. The books were Paxton Quigley's *Armed and Female*, Alan Gottlieb's *The Gun Grabbers*, and William Tonso's *The Gun Culture and Its Enemies*. The library, which has numerous branches, gratefully accepted the books.

Another hard-working group, the Keystone Second Amendment Association put 130 books in 17 high school, public, and college libraries in Clearfield County, Pennsylvania.

Second Amendment Foundation will be delighted to work with you in library donation projects. SAF can provide you the books at cost (about 1/3 to 1/2 of the retail price). They may be able to supply some books for free.

Libraries are also happy to have magazine subscriptions donated to them. The NRA magazine *American Rifleman* is a good choice. *InSights*, the NRA magazine for junior shooters, is a fine selection for school libraries. Because *InSights* is sent to so many schools, it has no political content. Some smaller libraries will accept your own copy of a magazine, once you're done with it. You can just cross out your name on the subscription label.

Some libraries, particularly small ones that cater to students writing reports for school, keep folders on current events such as gun control (which is a consistently popular student paper topic). The folders may include pamphlets, newspaper clips, and other miscellaneous materials. Ask the librarian if there is such a file, and if you can donate materials for it. The Research Reports and NRA/ILA brochures mentioned in chapter 1 would be good items to include.

Libraries usually have community bulletin boards, as do organizations such as the American Legion and the Veterans of Foreign Wars. Keep an eye on the bulletin boards and, if the public is allowed to post materials, stick up a flyer from your local pro-rights organization.

Some libraries set up table displays from time to time. If you see that your library has one, consider offering to set one up about gun control. Before speaking with the librarian, examine what other kinds of displays the library has, and try to design something that fits in with what the library is already used to. The librarian will probably be more receptive if you can provide a balanced set of materials, rather than information that just reflects the pro-rights viewpoint. Don't worry about letting the public see the other side; the pro-rights argument, when examined in a logical and careful manner, is so much more persuasive than the gun control side that moving the public debate away from emotions and towards reason nearly always makes converts for the Second Amendment.

The above advice about advance preparation fits in for just about everything mentioned in this book: *Advance scouting is always a good idea.* Before you write a letter to the editor of the local paper, read the letters to the editor column, and see what kind of letters get printed. Before you visit a Congresswoman's office, study her voting record.

Not every place where people sit for hours and hours reading old magazines is called a "library." Some such places are called "the doctor's waiting room." Waiting rooms are an excellent place to leave pro-rights magazines such as the *American Rifleman.* Make sure to cross out your name, so some well-intentioned soul doesn't mail it back to you, thinking you left it in the waiting room by mistake. Doctors, dentists, barbers, hairdressers, auto mechanics, and lots of other professionals all have waiting rooms full of customers desperate for something to read that's more interesting (and accurate) than a six-month-old issue of *Time.*

3. *Letters to the Editor*

"To the press alone, checquered as it is with abuses, the world is indebted for all the triumphs which have been gained by reason and humanity over error and oppression."
—Thomas Jefferson, Virginia and Kentucky
Resolutions, 1799.

One of the best things a gun rights defender can do is write letters to the editor of his or her local newspaper.

More people read letters to the editor than read the editorials written by professional columnists. Letters to the editor are a unique chance to influence thousands of people.

How to Do It

One excuse people offer for not writing is "I'm not a good writer" or "I don't know enough to write." Well, you don't have to be an outstanding scribe to get published in the local newspaper. If you have even a minimal amount of common sense, you have what it takes to write a good letter. After all, you understand the right to bear arms better than do the people who write for *Newsweek* and the *Los Angeles Times*. Much of what those "professional" writers do is reprint propaganda from Handgun Control Inc. You can do better than that.

Free literature available from the NRA and the Second Amendment Foundation will give you all the data you need for a good short letter. (The free literature is discussed in chapter 1.)

Your hometown newspaper may be biased against guns in its news and editorial sections, but that doesn't exclude you from getting a good letter printed. Many editorial pages welcome letters that challenge the viewpoint in the rest of the newspaper.

Here are some key words to remember when composing your letter. If you keep these words in mind, you'll get published:

25

Short. 100 words or less. That's enough time to convey one or two ideas. Long letters have a much smaller chance of being published. Even if you're responding to a long diatribe against guns, stick to one or two important points, rather than trying to rebut everything.

Type the letter. This isn't mandatory, but it does help. Otherwise, write long-hand. In either case, double space.

Clear. Express a forceful opinion on one side of the issue. Don't waffle. This one should be easy.

Prejudiced. Don't be. Never say anything that is racist, sexist, homophobic, or displays any other prejudice. Prejudice instantly kills a letter, and brings all gun owners into disrepute.

Focus. Emphasize our positive side. Tell the people the facts which support our case. Avoid personal attacks on opponents.

Tact. Honey catches more flies than vinegar. For example, if a news story misstates the facts about guns, you letter doesn't have to start out: "Your rotten paper has once again proven that it is a biased mouthpiece for bleeding-heart liberal Commies." Instead, the letter can gently offer to "clarify" a point that wasn't fully discussed in the news article. The softer you talk, the better people can hear you.

One at a time. If you're lucky enough to live in a town with two competing daily newspapers (there are only 16 such cities left), only write to one paper at a time. Add a p.s. note to your letter saying that you are sending the letter to only this paper. Papers prefer that their material be exclusive. Wait ten days, and if you don't hear from the first paper, send the letter to the other paper.

Wait. Here's one situation where a waiting period actually does some good. If you've been published in a paper recently, wait 30 days before sending another letter to the same paper.

The Letters to the Editor section is a community forum; papers don't want any one person to appear too often.

Address and phone number should be included at the top of the page. Papers often call to confirm a letter before printing.

Peg. Hang your letter on a news peg. This is very important. If you write a letter in response to a recent news story or editorial, the paper will be more likely to print it. There's nothing the media loves so much as printing stories about the media. Even criticism of the media gets lots of print space, since (from the viewpoint of the media, four-year-olds, and similar types) negative attention is way better than no attention at all.

Sign the letter. Never send an anonymous letter. Nor should you sign your letter "Ed Barnhill, NRA Member." The fact that you're an NRA member won't make the letter more persuasive to people who didn't agree with you already. If you want to add something to the signature block, add something that will show the readers that you're a responsible member of the community, e.g. "retired teacher, farmer, homemaker, doctor, etc." (Don't sign the letter "Ed Barnhill, etc.," unless your name is actually "Ed Barnhill, etc..")

Finally, write the letter so that a person who didn't read the original article can still follow your argument. For example, a letter might read:

> *A recent editorial ("Stop the Slaughter," April 22) claimed that "Drug dealers can walk into a store and walk out five minutes later with a machine gun, no questions asked." Actually, no-one can buy a machine gun in five minutes.*
> *Five months is more like it. Machine guns have been strictly regulated by federal law since 1934. To buy any fully automatic firearm, a person needs to get a federal license which*

requires fingerprints and a background check, and takes many months of paperwork.

Before we enact even more gun controls, people should understand how many we already have.

If you follow these ten rules, about 1 in 5 of your letters will get published. That's a success rate to be proud of, and you'll be making an important contribution to the debate.

Your chances of being published, by the way, are better in smaller newspapers, since there's less competition from other writers. The odds you will get published in the *New York Times* are better than the odds that you will get struck by lightening— but not a lot better. Your prospects in the *Staten Island Advance* are much better, and your odds in a smaller paper are better still. And remember, it's the readers of the smaller papers who, since they're more likely to live in smaller cities, may be more receptive to the pro-rights message.

Advanced Techniques

While the above rules are mandatory (if you want to get published), below are some suggestions that, although not essential, will be helpful.

Newspapers are written by generalists, who understandably cannot familiarize themselves with every issue. Thus, reporters and editors look for material from people who are well-known experts on a particular subject. In the letter-to-the-editor context, your letter will be more persuasive to the editor (and likely to get printed) if you can cite authoritative sources.

For example, the sentence "gun control never works" is merely an assertion. More persuasive is the sentence "According to the Wright-Rossi study for the National Institute of Justice, there is no evidence that any current gun controls have worked."

Likewise, instead of saying "The authors of the Constitution supported an individual right to bear arms," supply a one-sentence quote from James Madison or Thomas Jefferson discussing the individual right.

Alternatively, when you offer a statistic, put the source of the statistic in parenthesis: "While Mr. Meddlethorpe claims that 'the record murder rate proves the need for gun control,' the murder rate today is lower than it was in 1981. (FBI Uniform Crime Reports.)" Don't worry if citing authority makes the letter a little too long; the editors can always cut it if they want.

And it's all right to bring in personal experience. Newspapers always like printing "eyewitness" accounts; so if one of the reasons that you think semiautomatics should remain legal is that you frightened off a burglar with one, tell your story.

Newspapers love to find inconsistencies—two government agencies undercutting each other's work, or a Senator's actions contradicting his words. So if you can find an inconsistency and point it out, go right ahead.

As with every other thing you write, the first sentence is the most important, so write it carefully.

Make a copy for yourself to keep (but if you don't have ready access to a copy machine, just mail the letter, rather than letting it sit in your jacket pocket for ten days until you find a photocopier).

Mail the letter the day *after* you write it. Letting it cool gives you time to retract any intemperate remarks, and gives you an extra day to think about the letter, and perhaps find some refinements. As Thomas Paine observed, the best writing comes from warm passions and a cool temper.

Does it Matter?

Even letters that don't get published make a positive impact. The young newspaper staffer who is in charge of editing the letters to the editor page will one day be running her own editorial page at some newspaper. Your letter may be one of the few pro-gun arguments she is exposed to all year.

Most media types don't hate guns out of genuine conviction. It's simply a cultural prejudice of their environment. Some people, if exposed to the facts, will gradually reconsider their viewpoint.

Like everything else in the paper, published letters to the editor are also read by the rest of the newspaper's staff, including reporters and editors. Letters about a particular subject may convince the reporters and editors that the gun issue is important to the readership, and deserves thorough, frequent coverage.

Will a published letter really matter? You bet. A 1989 issue of the *Yale Law Journal* contained an article by Sanford Levinson called "The Embarrassing Second Amendment." Levinson, one of the top Constitutional law professors in the US, wrote that liberal academics (himself included) should face up to the overwhelming evidence: The Second Amendment really does guarantee an individual right to bear arms.

Levinson's article dealt a tremendous blow to the silly theory that the Second Amendment is only a guarantee that states can have a National Guard. (The theory never caught on with ordinary people, but had been popular in the academic community.) Professor Levinson's piece cites a number of letters to the editor of ordinary newspapers. In fact, it was Levinson's reading of letters in his local newspaper that made him realize that huge numbers of people really care about the Second Amendment—even though most law professors don't. Levinson began to consider that maybe the letter writers were right, and the law professors were wrong.

Professor Levinson isn't the only person influenced by letters to the editor. Except for the front page, the letters section is more widely read than any other part of the newspaper—even the editorial page.

Congressional staffers follow letters to the editor in the Congressperson's home-town newspapers as an important gauge of public opinion back home.

Although Congressional staffers will likely have read your published letter, send them a copy anyway. If your letter praised the Congressperson, send her a copy, even if it wasn't printed. She'll appreciate the fact that gun owners are standing by her, and will therefore be more likely to stand by them.

Op-ed Pieces

Once you've established a good track record as a letter writer, consider trying to write opinion pieces for your local paper.

The general rules discussed above for letters apply for most op-eds too. Total length should be 650-750 words. Going even slightly above the limit seriously impairs your chance of getting published.

Before submitting a piece, call your newspaper's opinion page, and ask for their guidelines regarding op-ed submissions.

If you're a university or high school student, your situation is somewhat easier, since most school newspapers are eager to publish student writers.

4. Talk Radio

"THE TANK, THE B-52, THE FIGHTER-BOMBER, THE
STATE CONTROLLED POLICE ARE THE WEAPONS OF
DICTATORSHIP. THE RIFLE IS THE WEAPON OF
DEMOCRACY...IF GUNS ARE OUTLAWED, ONLY THE
GOVERNMENT WILL HAVE GUNS. ONLY THE POLICE,
THE SECRET POLICE, THE MILITARY, THE HIRED SER-
VANTS OF OUR RULERS. ONLY THE GOVERNMENT AND
A FEW OUTLAWS. I INTEND TO BE AMONG THE
OUTLAWS."   —Edward Abbey.

The suggestions below are written for callers, but are equally applicable to guests.

Listen to the show for a while, so you can get a sense of the show's style and direction.

Many of the points made about letters to newspapers (chapter 3) or letters to Congress (chapter 15) apply here too. Don't get mad, don't scream, don't use obscenities. Negative behavior simply turns off the listening audience, and convinces people that gun owners really are mentally dangerous.

You'll be nervous the first few times you call, but with practice, you'll get more confident and relaxed.

Convincing the host is not the objective; he's already made his mind up. Your goal is to get a little bit of air time to present some facts to the radio audience.

Make specific factual points, not just vague generalizations. Alan's *Gun Rights Fact Book* (see page 4) includes a section of suggested talking points for radio call-ins.

Try to make your points in about 30 seconds or less. Don't read long quotations (like the one at the start of this chapter).

Remember that the host (or the studio guest) will always have the last word. Don't let this discourage you. Even if the host or guest argues with some of the points you've made, you will still have helped bring some people in the radio audience over to our side.

Similarly, the host may interrupt you. Don't get insulted. It's his show, and he has to keep things moving with the timing he feels best.

The host may try to agitate you, to provoke you into an angry response. Fireworks build the host's rating, but they don't do our cause any good. So no matter what, stay cool under pressure.

Listen to the callers who come ahead of you. Maybe you'll have something to say to support a comment by a pro-gun caller, or to refute a comment from an anti.

Never engage in name-calling with the host or another caller, even if they start it. Instead of calling someone a "liar," explain how they're mistaken.

Some shows are limited to a specific subject, usually related to the show's guest. On a specific subject show, you of course have to confine your comments to that day's subject matter.

In contrast, other shows are "open forum." The host solicits call-ins to discuss anything they want. You can often get a lively discussion going about gun control.

If you bring up the gun issue and the host of an open forum show doesn't want to talk about it, don't take it personally. The gun debate gets a lot of exposure on talk radio, and some hosts may think that they need to force a broader variety of topics.

And most importantly: Be nice. A large fraction of the listeners will be paying more attention to your overall tone than to your specific points.

If you don't know the answer to a question, say so, and move on to another topic.

One tactic used by our opponents is for one of them to call a radio station and pretend to be an irate NRA member who favors gun control. To weed out the callers who claim to be NRA members but aren't, bring a copy of the most recent *American Rifleman* or *American Hunter* to the studio with you, and have a question ready about it. (E.g. "If you're really an NRA member, can you name just one feature article in the latest issue of the magazine?"). If the host is pro-rights, you might want to inform him in advance about the fake NRA caller problem.

Citizens Band Radio

Who says that broadcast radio is the only way to get the message out? CB-er Charles Howell broadcasts short pro-gun messages on his radio, informing them about the latest in gun control news.

The CB audience is especially important, he notes, because it includes so many truckers. Lots of truckers own guns, but because they're on the road for weeks at a time, they may be cut off from regular news sources.

Truckers enjoy the unenviable status of being one of the many groups of American even more harassed by excessive government than are gun-owners. So truckers understand the importance of limited government.

5. *Read Gun Week*

"EVERY GOOD AND EXCELLENT THING STANDS MO-
MENT BY MOMENT ON THE RAZOR EDGE OF DANGER
AND MUST BE FOUGHT FOR." —Thornton Wilder.

Lack of information can be dangerous to you and your gun rights. The general media do not do an adequate job of giving an objective description of gun-related events and statistics. Whether it's the federal scene, or states and cities, there is no other way to get the crucial information as fast as subscribing to a publication dedicated to firearms information.

If you didn't hear about a gun control proposal in Congress until your local paper reported the outcome of a Congressional vote, then you haven't been reading *Gun Week*. *Gun Week* keeps you posted on what the gun control lobby is doing before it is too late for you to do something. Regular reports from Washington DC keeps you up to date on federal issues, but *Gun Week* also reports on what is happening at state capitals around the country. Every week *Gun Week* tells you what you need to know to protect your gun rights.

Regular hunting reports are also a valuable part of your *Gun Week* subscription. Deer, elk, turkey, bear, waterfowl, upland birds, small game—*Gun Week* covers all the seasons. Most importantly, *Gun Week* covers the seasons on a regional and local level. When deer season in Pennsylvania looks terrific, elk hunting in Colorado looks so-so, or Michigan has just issued new hunting regulations, you'll read about it in *Gun Week*.

Gun Week's new product reviews evaluate new outdoor products before you shell out your hard-earned money. Every week you can read reports about new clothing, handguns, rifles, sights, knives, powders, ammunition and anything that can make you a better hunter or shooter. *Gun Week* is also the first and best place to look for important product recalls that increase your safety.

Gun Week has been leading the media pack on industry news as well. Do you know about the metallurgical problems with the M-9 pistol, or the FBI's struggles to adopt a new semiautomatic, or the troubles at Glock? If none of this sounds familiar then you haven't been reading *Gun Week*.

A year's subscription costs $32.00, just $.64 per issue, which is probably less than the cup of coffee you get at the local diner. And there is no risk of disappointment; if you are not 100% satisfied you will be promptly refunded for unmailed issues—no questions asked, no hard feelings. You simply can't go wrong. In fact, you will probably wonder how you ever got along without it.

You can subscribe by calling the Second Amendment Foundation at 1-206-454-7012.

A few years ago, one of Rep. Charles Schumer's Brooklyn constituents bought him a gift subscription to *Gun Week*. Schumer was so upset that he wrote back, and asked to have the subscription canceled.

Most Congresspeople, however, are not as frightened of open debate as Rep. Schumer is. A trial subscription sent to your Senator, or State Representative, or City Councilwoman probably won't turn them into NRA Life Members. But it may show some of them a new perspective.

And just maybe, some college intern in the office will read *Gun Week* with an open mind, and come to some new conclusions about the right to bear arms.

6. The Big Lie, or Don't Believe Everything You Read

"No matter how thin you slice it, it's still baloney." —New York Governor Alfred E. Smith, speech, 1936.

Handgun Control, Inc. knows how effective pro-rights grassroots lobbyists are. That's why HCI has invented a special campaign, "Operation Alienate," designed to drive gun owners away from the NRA and other pro-rights organizations. What HCI hopes is that if you read enough negative information about the right to bear arms and its supporters, you'll stop working to defend your rights.

In fact, much of the anti-gun "information" you read in the press is really disinformation—falsehoods invented by the anti-gun lobbies, and thoughtlessly repeated by the media.

The problem of media disinformation is not limited to the gun issue. During the Persian Gulf War, University of Massachusetts sociologists Sut Jhally, Justin Lewis, and Michael Morgan tested people for their knowledge of important facts about the conflict (e.g. knowledge that Kuwait was not a democracy). The authors found that the more television people watched, the *less* they knew. That is, after controlling for other variables, the study discovered that people who watched a lot of television coverage of the war knew less about the war than people who watched only a little television.

In the gun issue, who's telling the truth. The NRA and Handgun Control, Inc. both accuse each other of being fundamentally dedicated to dishonesty. At least one of the two organizations must be lying quite a bit. Here's what *Library Journal* said in its Sept. 15, 1988 "Alarums and Diversions" column: "A highly placed library source in Washington, D.C. told A&D that the American Library Association lobby and the National Rifle Association lobby are the only ones whose information was considered consistently truthful and reliable by legislators."

So before you let some hysterical article in the national media drive you out of the guns rights movement, take the latest anti-gun screed with a big grain of salt.

7. Computer Bulletin Boards

"NECESSITY IS THE PLEA OF EVERY INFRINGEMENT OF
HUMAN FREEDOM. IT IS THE ARGUMENT OF TYRANTS;
IT IS THE CREED OF SLAVES."
—William Pitt, English statesman
and friend of American independence,
Speech on the India Bill, Nov. 18, 1783.

If your personal computer has a modem (short for "modulator/demodulator"), the computer can communicate over phone lines with other computers.

If you don't have a modem, you can buy either an internal modem (a circuit board that goes into one of your computer's expansion slots) or an external modem (which is attached to one of the serial ports at the back of your computer). In either case, the modem has two phone jacks in it, one of which runs to your telephone, the other of which runs to the wall jack (where the telephone line from outside enters the room).

Modems require communications software to run them; almost every modem vendor will supply you with software too.

The faster a modem, the more it costs. However, speedy modems will usually pay for themselves in the long run by saving you long distance charges (since they transmit data faster). Try to get a modem rated at least at 2400 bps, with 9600 being preferable (and increasingly affordable).

Anyway, once you've got a working modem, you can— using the communications software—instruct the modem to connect over the telephone lines with another computer that is ready to receive phone calls. You can then communicate with any other computer that also has a modem. For instance, you can dial your cousin Egbert's computer (assuming that he has a modem, and has his communications software on and ready to receive calls), and send him your file containing chocolate chip cookie recipes. Or better (from a gun rights point of view), you can dial a gun rights bulletin board.

A bulletin board is a computer that is dedicated to making itself available for communication with other computers. A bulletin board contains files, electronic mail, and other material of use to the people who dial in to the bulletin board. There are literally tens of thousands of bulletin boards in the United States, covering a huge diversity of topics. Below is a list of bulletin boards focusing on the right to bear arms.

All bulletin boards listed under state headings belong to the "Paul Revere Network" run by Leroy Pyle, and all Paul Revere boards echo each other; this means that if a file becomes available on one Paul Revere board, it will shortly become available on all Paul Revere boards.

Pro-rights bulletin boards transmit information instantaneously. They are unquestionably the fastest way to get in-depth information about gun rights issues around the nation.

The boards also have "conferences," which are discussion areas for particular topics, such as reloading. Conference participants can write messages to each other, and leave the messages for viewing in the conference area. Thus, they can have a discussion stretching over weeks and months, without having to be sending their messages at the same time.

The bulletin board listing below is arranged by state. For all of these boards, your modem settings should be N-8-1.

Arizona
Brass Cannon. (602) 639-1039.
Run-Time. (602) 779-3115. PRN

Arkansas
Conway PC Users Group. (501) 329-7227.

California
The Silhouetter. (209) 472-0843.
PRN Los Angeles. (310) 837-7818.
Telecommuter WorkSystems. (310) 676-0492.
Paul Revere Network Headquarters. (408) 947-9800.
PRNet/SF Eastbay. (510) 791-8246.
The City of Tanelorn. (510) 803-0319.
Rights of the People. (619) 961-1708.
A&B Express. (619) 447-0641.

Eagle's Nest. (818) 769-6584.
Bullet Box. (818) 403-0399.
NRA/ILA Sacramento. (916) 446-3221.
Highsierra Online. (916) 577-4438.

Florida
RedMan. (305) 435-1972.

Minnesota
Minnesota MinuteMan. (612) 493-3558.

Missouri
Party Line. (314) 845-7937.
PRN Central. (816) 597-3950.
The Institute. (816) 421-3944.
The Money Pit. (913) 287-1102.

New Hampshire
The Quiet Revolution. (603) 753-9716.
VAXCAT. (603) 424-023.

New York
Airpower Rybbs. (215)- 259-2198.
ImageSoft. (516) 767-5189.
Midnite Caller. (716) 297-0291.
Knights of Discovery. (716) 837-2901.
The Outback. (914) 339-1816.
Paul Revere Network. (914) 339-1816.
The Network. (914) 635-9501.
The Rifle Range. (914) 452-4753.
PRN/DIS. (914) 635-2712.
Ghandeel's Fortress. (914) 647-7280.
The Final Encyclopedia. (914) 737-2539.

Ohio
PRN Cincinnati. (513) 474-9193.
Liberty Line. (513) 891-2430.
The Christian Star. (614) 841-9991.

Oklahoma
Gunners Mate. (918) 665-6841.
Bedrock. (918) 985-6836.

Oregon
The Post House. (503) 667-2649.

Pennsylvania
2nd Amendment. (814) 898-1732.

South Carolina
Schroedinger's Catbox. (803) 652-3759.

Tennessee
Southern Cross. (615) 349-5473.
Reality Relief Fido. (615) 690-2227.
Reality's Link. (615) 246-5595.

Texas
The Firing Line. (214) 341-5582.
BackStage. (409) 721-9606. PRN
Flotom Ent. (512) 282-3941.
Jack's Range. (915) 757-9311. PRN

Virginia
Bullet 'n Board. (703) 971-4491. PRN
PRN/LGC. (804) 877-8320.

Washington
Troubador Systems. (206) 661-2135.

National
Of all the pro-rights boards, the best one is Gun Talk, run by NRA/ILA. The number is 1-703-719-6406.

To register as a user, you need to supply your NRA membership number, and pay a $15 annual fee (to defray part of the enormous hardware costs associated with operating a BBS with numerous incoming phone lines capable of operating simultaneously). You can register on-line, or by calling 1-800-GUN-TALK.

Once you're registered, you have full access to the Gun Talk BBS, with no further fees (except of course long-distance charges from wherever you're calling).

The opening menu of Gun Talk offers you the option of reading any of about two dozen bulletins dealing with up-to-minute accounts of key political battles, recent news involving gun issues, and fast-breaking legislative developments.

A Files Section contains several hundred text files dealing with every angle of the right to bear arms issue. Historical articles about the original meaning of the Second Amendment; detailed analysis of topical issues such as waiting periods; reprints of articles from *American Rifleman*, *American Hunter*, and the popular media; ballistics tables; and much, much more are all available in the Files Section.

The Files Section can be a tremendous resource when you need hard facts to put in a letter to the editor or to an elected official.

Finally, Gun Talk allows you to send messages to other Gun Talk users. While you can send private messages to an individual, almost all messages are intended for public consumption, and are posted in a Message Section for all to read. The contents of the Messages Section are as diverse as the users, and include debates about the recent Presidential race, questions about reloading technique and gun repair, updates on forthcoming gun shows, and first-hand reports about what it's really like to try to get a pistol license in New York.

Another national BBS paying attention to gun rights issue is the Outdoor Forum, on Compuserve. The Forum is shared by a number of hunting and outdoor groups.

Canada

Canadian bulletin boards dealing in part with firearms or the right to bear arms:

CARS—The Automotive BBS (Alberta). (403) 752-3930.
K9COPS BBS (British Columbia). (604) 599-0514.
Yorkton Area Opus (Saskatchewan). (306) 782-1355.

8. Telephone Hotlines

"NOBODY MAKES A GREATER MISTAKE THAN HE WHO
DOES NOTHING BECAUSE HE COULD ONLY DO A
LITTLE." —Edmund Burke

Recorded telephone hotlines are one of the best sources
for up-to-date information about gun control battles. You can
call evenings or weekends, if you want to reduce long-distance
charges. Besides the normal phone charge, there is no fee for
calling any of these numbers, except as noted below.

National
Neal Knox's Firearms Coalition runs a high-quality automated
phone message center. The messages are usually updated once
or twice a week. 301-871-3006.

International
Sporting Shooters Association of Australia. Dial Australia, then
0055 23308. This number is similar to a 900 number; besides
long-distance charges, you also pay a premium to the phone
company of up to 70 cents per minute. The SSAA earns revenue
from the service.

California
California Rifle & Pistol Association. (800)-I'M 4 GUNS (800-
464-4867). This 800 number is only usable from within California.
Gun Owners ACTION Committee. 714-871-4515.

Colorado
Firearms Coalition. 303-369-GUNS.

Connecticut
Coalition of Connecticut Sportsmen. 203-722-3030.

Massachusetts
Sportsmen's Legislative Hotline. (800) 338-6999. (Only from

within Massachusetts.)

Missouri
Western Missouri Shooters' Alliance. (816) 444-0228.

Texas
Texas State Rifle Association. (512) 288-3242.
North Texas Arms Rights Coalition (214) 270-4068.

9. Attend a Leadership Training Seminar

"Parum proficet scire fieri debel, si non
cognoscus quomodo sit facturum."
(Roman legal maxim: "It profits little to know
what ought to be done, if you do not know
how it is to be done.")

If you want to be a part of the gun rights movement, then eventually you must meet with other members and leaders of the movement. Fortunately, with the gun rights movement this is easy to do.

Gun Rights Policy Conference

Each year, the major players in the gun rights movement gather at an event called the Gun Rights Policy Conference. Together with activists from across the nation, as well as local participants, each year's activities are reviewed, and strategies shared. The Gun Rights Policy Conference provides you with an inside scope view of how the gun rights movement operates, and lets you become a part of that process.

Since 1986 the annual meeting, which is free to the public, has been sponsored by the Second Amendment Foundation, the Citizens Committee for the Right to Keep and Bear Arms and *Gun Week* newspaper. In addition, over 40 other organizations and industry leaders provide funding or other types of support to the conference. The GRPC has gained the attention of the national media for its ability to draw together all of the heavy hitters in the pro-gun movement.

The GRPC is the largest meeting of its kind in America. Registration for the event has risen steadily each year as more people experience the benefits of attending the conference. As a result, opportunities abound for interested individuals to talk face-to-face with the people who are on the front lines and in the headlines.

The schedule for the GRPC is spread out over two nights and three days. Participants are free to select which events to attend as receptions, speeches, panel discussions and other meetings give everyone the opportunity to participate fully.

Make your plans to attend the next Gun Rights Policy Conference by contacting the Second Amendment Foundation, 12500 NE 10th Place, Bellevue, WA 98005. 1-206-454 7012.

Attend a Leadership Training Conference

If you cannot attend the Gun Rights Policy Conference the next best thing to do is attend a Leadership Training Conference held by the Citizens Committee for the Right to Keep and Bear Arms. These meetings are much smaller both in size and scope than the GRPC, but the lessons learned are no less valuable.

Leadership Training Conferences are one day events where the focus is on intensive training in the art of grass roots lobbying. The speakers and materials aim to assist motivated individuals in becoming effective voices in the gun rights movement. Topics include means to affect the outcome of legislative deliberations, organizing a local gun rights organization, successful fund raising, organizing a communications network and other aspects of the daily fight to save our firearms rights from extinction.

Make your plans to attend the next Leadership Training Conference in your area by contacting the Projects Director at the Citizens Committee for the Right to Keep and Bear Arms 12500 NE 10th Place, Bellevue, WA 98005. 1-206-454-4911.

10. Speeches and Debates

"GUARD WITH JEALOUS ATTENTION THE PUBLIC LIB-
ERTY. SUSPECT EVERYONE WHO APPROACHES THAT
JEWEL."   —Patrick Henry.

Style

Begin to establish a bond with the audience by relating an experience of your own which the audience is likely to have shared.

Wear a suit and tie (just a suit, if you're female). Surveys of college students show that they have more intellectual respect for professors who dress professionally, rather than the ones who dress casually.

Instead of writing the speech word for word, jot down key words and topics that you can glance at as you go along. It's much more fun to hear somebody who's speaking instead of somebody who's reading aloud. Keep your sentences short, remembering that things presented orally must be simpler than things delivered in writing. Make sure that your speech has a beginning, a middle, and a conclusion. Maintain eye contact with the audience as much as possible. Instead of looking over the audience's heads, focus on one particular person, and speak directly to her. Of course make sure to keep changing the person you focus on. Practice, practice, practice your speech before you deliver it to the audience.

One obvious audience for speeches is gun clubs or hunting clubs. But don't overlook other potential audiences. For example, groups such as Rotary Clubs have weekly luncheon meetings, always with a new speaker. Same for the Kiwanis, for women's clubs, and for the League of Women Voters. Many would be glad to have someone address their group about a topic in the news.

And bring along some written materials to hand out to interested people afterwards. Membership flyers from your local gun rights group are a good choice, as is any of the educational material discussed above in Chapter 1.

Substance

Choose *one* topic for a short speech. It's much easier to write a good, powerful speech on a single subject, than to try to cover the whole field. A single topic might be "The Truth about So-called Assault Weapons" or "What the Second Amendment Means" or "Why Concealed Carry Permit Laws Are a Good Idea" or "Why Waiting Periods Don't Work" or "Because the Police have no Legal Obligation to Protect Individuals, People Need the Ability to Protect Themselves."

In addition, gear the topic to the audience. If you're speaking for a gun club, the audience might appreciate a fairly "advanced" topic, such as how waiting periods set the stage for gun prohibition. In contrast, an audience of Rotarians might want an elementary introduction to the Second Amendment, or a discussion of the importance of self-defense and responsible gun ownership in today's high-crime society.

As with virtually every other type of persuasive communication, concrete examples work well. If you're talking about waiting periods, discuss the people who couldn't get a gun to defend their families during the Los Angeles riots because of California's 15-day waiting period.

Debates

Most of the same rules applicable to speeches apply to debates as well. One major difference is that you'll have much less time to develop your points.

In debates (and in general), try to stay focused on the pro-rights positive agenda, instead of attempting to rebut point-by-point every argument made by your opponent. If your debate opponents says something like "The gun nuts want semi-automated plastic machine guns firing cop-killer teflon bullets to be sold to children without a waiting period," it would take you 15 minutes to rebut each of the charges contained in the single sentence.

Instead, keep the debate on our positive issues, with which the vast majority of people agree with us: using force to defend home and family is morally legitimate; because the police cannot protect everyone, people should have the option to protect themselves; criminals are afraid of and deterred by armed citizens; gun controls affect only criminals, and distract politicians from genuine solutions to crime.

Except in front of an audience of lawyers or similar group, don't spend a lot of time on Constitutional issues. You can make the point that your own state Constitution (in most states) as well as the federal Constitution guarantee a right to bear arms, and the US Supreme Court re-affirmed the individual right in the 1990 *Verdugo-Urquidez* case. But in general, non-lawyer audiences are more likely to be persuaded by practical arguments than by legal ones.

11. Look Good on TV

"THERE ARE NOT ENOUGH JAILS, NOT ENOUGH PO-
LICEMEN, NOT ENOUGH COURTS TO ENFORCE A LAW
NOT SUPPORTED BY THE PEOPLE."
— Vice-President Hubert H. Humphrey,
speech, Williamsburg, Virginia, May 1, 1965.

When gun control stories are happening, television stations often come to local gun stores for interviews and pictures. Sometimes the media uses the gun store footage for anti-gun purposes.

A typical anti-gun segment might show a police chief calling for "strict gun control" and offering some phony statistic. Then the announcer would say, "But not everyone agrees." The picture then shifts to a gun store owner with a two-day old beard and a ratty shirt, claiming that "Gun control is just a conspiracy of the damn liberals."

Viewers who are making up their minds about the issue will find the neat and clean police chief much more convincing than the slovenly store owner.

So if you get a request for an interview, accept *only* if can make sure that you and your surroundings (such as your body and/or gun store) are neat and tidy before the cameras roll. And *only* if you feel confident that you know enough about the particular issue to speak persuasively. It's no disgrace modestly to step aside, and suggest someone else who you know to be a good talker. It is a disgrace to put your ego ahead of the pro-rights cause, and do a bad job when someone else could have done a good job.

Preparing your Substance

Before the television appearance, watch as many segments of the program as you can. Write down about four key points you want to convey. The purpose of writing isn't for you to read out loud later, but to help you organize your thoughts. Think up concrete examples that support your point.

55

Even if the interviewer is sympathetic to your point of view, he or she will try to ask you challenging questions. That's how journalists conceive their job. So during your preparation work, think of the hardest questions that someone could ask. And think of the questions that someone might asked, based on the other side's main arguments. Then think up responses to all those hard questions. Have a friend play the role of interviewer, and ask you tough questions.

One good way to handle hostile questions is to use them as a transition to the positive points you want to make. That way, instead of being on the defensive, you're communicating a positive agenda.

For example, if the question is "Why do you support the availability of these assault weapons which drug dealers like so much?" the answer could be "Actually those guns are hardly ever used by criminals. Most of the folks who like semiautomatics are target shooters, or people who want a reliable home-defense firearm."

Preparing your Appearance

As we keep suggesting throughout this book in regards to public appearances, dress conservatively, preferably in a business suit. *Never* dress in hunting clothes, camouflage, or carry a gun. Even if the station asks you to. The station's interest in sensationalism is outweighed by your interest in looking dignified.

For television, there are also a couple other clothing suggestions. The ideal men's shirt is a light blue one, and the ideal tie is a conservative one. If you're a male with long hair or beard, follow your mother's advice (just this once), and get it neatly trimmed.

If your ego is too big to let a barber tidy up your beard a little, then you're putting your personal satisfaction ahead of everyone else's freedom.

During the 1968 New Hampshire Democratic Presidential primary, Senator Eugene McCarthy was helped tremendously by the thousands of young people who came to New Hampshire to support his insurgent campaign against President

Lyndon Johnson. The youthful volunteers were mainly moti-vated by McCarthy's strong stand against the Vietnam War, and the volunteers, similar to like-minded youth of the era, sported thick beards and long hair. And the men were even more far-out!

Yet when these "long-haired" rebels headed off to conservative New Hampshire to campaign door-to-door, they got haircuts, following their motto "Clean for Gene." Their objective was to help Gene McCarthy beat Lyndon Johnson; and if it required a haircut to avoid alienating New Hampshire voters, they got a haircut.

And on primary day, little-known, underfinanced Sena-tor Eugene McCarthy garnered a stunning 42% of the New Hampshire vote. Within weeks, President Johnson withdrew his bid for re-election. Going "Clean for Gene" had knocked out an incumbent President.

So if a 1968 hippie was willing to get a crew cut, you can at least ask the barber to trim your beard a little.

Television stations generally won't offer to apply makeup, but if you arrive early and ask for it, they might put some on for you. Makeup is helpful, but not at all essential, particularly with modern studio lighting, which is much less likely to make you sweat than its predecessors from a couple decades ago.

Women can continue to use whatever makeup they feel comfortable with already, as long as it's not excessive. Use lipstick and eye liner sparingly.

If any of jewelry is larger than "small," leave it at home. Jangly jewelry will distract the viewers.

Women's clothes should emphasize soft colors. Big prints, big polka dots, bold stripes, and giant checked patterns are out. So are pure black, pure white, and pure black and white. Ideally, your suit, skirt, or dress should come below the knee. Pants are okay too, and should also go below the knee.

While dressing conservatively, still pick out clothes that you're comfortable in and familiar with.

Obviously there are a lot of television personalities who don't follow the above clothing guidelines, and who look great on TV. At the same time, there are a lot of television personalities who do follow these guidelines, and also look great. The guidelines aren't intended for Geraldo; they're intended to help someone who's *not* a professional TV person look their best the first time out. After you've done a dozen TV appearances, you'll have enough experience under your belt to figure out if you can vary the appearance guidelines a little.

And remember, gun control is a "hot button" issue, and the other side tries hard to whip up public hysteria. Our job in communicating with the public is to present the calm, rational side of things. If your appearance is conservative and dignified, it supports your message instead of distracting from it.

When the crew is done taping you, leave the interviewer a card or piece of paper with your name and phone number, in case they need to do any follow-up. When you get home, send thank-you notes to the television station's contact person, and to the interviewer.

On the Air

Keep your head steady. Don't bob it around, the way you do in normal conversation.

Maintain eye contact with the interviewer, not the camera.

If you're in a chair, sit up straight (but don't be rigid). Remember what your mother taught you about posture.

If a mike is clipped on your shirt or tie (which is common in many sitting interviews), don't play with it!

SMILE! And then smile some more. A somber face on television looks terrible. And on television, a small smile looks almost somber. So let out your natural enthusiasm with a bright smile. (At the same time, don't make it look forced or unnatural.)

And just as your face can convey your enthusiasm, so can your voice—not in an angry or frantic manner—but in a vibrant, positive way.

If you naturally talk with your hands and arms, keep on doing so. Television likes things that move.

Be nice. No matter how discourteous the interviewer may be to you, stay nice, and don't blow your cool. Remember,

you're trying to make a good impression on the folks in television land, who may notice how you act much more than what you say. If you stay calm while the interviewer works himself into a hissy fit, you'll score points for the good guys.

Being nice, by the way, doesn't mean you can't be assertive. You just have to be nice while doing it.

Before answering, pause for a couple or three seconds to organize your answer. If you're being taped for later broadcast, the station will edit out any pauses. If you're live on the air, you'll still sound better with good answers than with hurried ones.

If the interviewer or interviewers ask you several questions simultaneously, don't get flustered. This isn't a doctoral dissertation oral exam, and you don't have to answer every question. Answer the one that gives you the best opportunity to present your positive agenda.

Keep your answers to each question to three sentences or less. A good format is to give the main point, and then illustrate it with one example.

If you keep your answers short, the station will be more likely to use the points that *you* wanted to make. If you give rambling, lengthy answers, the station's editors might pick out the weakest or silliest statement you made, ignoring the good points that surrounded it.

And despite all the preparatory warnings above, relax. You've probably got a nice personality, a good mind, and a nice smile. Just let them shine through, and you'll be fine.

Finally, when you gather your family around the television to watch the fifteen minute interview that was taped, don't feel disappointed when only five seconds of you shows up on the air. Television stations routinely shoot far more material than they expect to use. The theory is by shooting a lot, they build themselves a margin of safety to ensure they'll have all the good material they need.

12. Confronting the Media

"THE BRAVE MAN INATTENTIVE TO HIS DUTY IS WORTH LITTLE MORE TO HIS COUNTRY THAN THE COWARD WHO DESERTS HER IN THE HOUR OF DANGER."
—General Andrew Jackson, speech to troops before the Battle of New Orleans, January 8, 1815.

In rare cases, the media may impose a black-out on the pro-gun viewpoint. This doesn't mean the kind of coverage typical of the *New York Times*, where the news articles are usually slanted against guns, and the in-house editorials are always anti-gun, but pro-gun op-eds pieces and letters-to-the-editor do appear from time to time. Instead, we're talking about newspapers like the *San Jose Mercury-News* or the *Minneapolis Star-Tribune*, which have from time to time shut the pro-rights viewpoint out entirely.

In cases of pervasive or systemic bias, ask for a meeting with the relevant person at the newspaper or broadcast station (the news editor, or the editorial page editor, or the person in charge of letters to the editor). Bring two or three well-informed people to the meeting, and bring extensive clips from the paper documenting the problem. (Or for broadcast media, written notes of particular problems with particular shows.) Also bring pro-gun articles and books to give to the newspaper as background information. (If you can, avoid books published by gun groups.)

While the meeting will certainly not turn an anti-gun newspaper into a pro-gun one, it might convince the paper to let some opposing viewpoints trickle into print once in a while.

If your efforts at reasonable dialogue hit a stone wall, hold a rally in front of the media outlet, decrying its bias. Make sure to invite all the other media outlets in town to attend. And make sure to have detailed documentation of the picketed outlet's bias available.

PART II

INFLUENCING GOVERNMENT

The battle in the arena of public opinion is a warm-up for the battle in the halls of government. Here's how you can stop the passage of laws restricting freedom, and promote reform of existing laws that infringe our rights.

PART II

INFLUENCING GOVERNMENT

13. Register Voters, Not Guns

"SO THEY COMMITTED THEMSELVES TO THE WILL OF
GOD AND RESOLVED TO PROCEED."
—William Bradford, *Plymouth Plantation* (1647).

Does Registering to Vote Matter?

Some people may tell you that voting by our side doesn't make a difference. Nonsense. Just ask Moody Stallings. Virginia State Senator Moody Stallings centered his re-election campaign with boasts about his attacks on the NRA. In November 1991, Stallings was defeated for re-election, thanks in large part to pro-rights volunteers who flocked to Stallings' opponent, and got out the vote.

Every single vote really does count. During the 1980s in California, over 21 local elections were decided by a single vote.

Even in Presidential elections, pro-gun voters can make a difference. In 1980 and 1988, the pro-gun vote swung Pennsylvania (and several other states) to Ronald Reagan and George Bush.

Some folks complain about the paperwork and bother involved in registration. The question to ask them is: "Would you rather register to vote, or register your guns?" Either we vote and win elections, or the other side wins, and national registration of all guns will become a reality.

When we don't win elections, we pay a heavy price.

In 1990, Senator Howard Metzenbaum helped push a bill banning semi-automatics through the Senate by pointing out that the NRA had failed to defeat him in 1988, despite his being a fierce opponent of gun rights.

New York Governor Mario Cuomo expressed the sentiment that shows why many politicians feel free to ignore the opinion of gun owners. He called people who opposed his mandatory seat belt law "NRA hunters who drink beer, don't vote and lie to their wives about where they were all weekend." Beer-drinking is your own business, and where you were this weekend is between you and your spouse. As an American citizen you have a duty to vote, and a duty to vote against politicians who want to destroy our rights.

(Cuomo, by the way, apologized for the slur on the NRA, although he never recanted his anti-gun positions.)

Finding Information about Registration

The starting point for every registration campaign is the county election commission or similar office. The Commission will have all the information you need about registration. Procedures vary a lot from state to state. The Commission will also probably have plenty of free "how to register" literature that you can take and distribute.

In addition to county election commissions, the Secretary of State's office (located in the capital city of each state) also has voter registration information. At the state government level, the Secretary of State (usually an elected official) is the person responsible for supervising elections.

Another source for registration information is the local League of Women Voters. You could also contact the Election Services Division, League of Women Voters Education Fund, 1730 M St. NW, Washington, DC 20036, (202) 429-1965. The League is, unfortunately, anti-gun, which will make it all the more satisfying to use its resources to elect pro-rights candidates.

Political parties are also an excellent place to go for registration assistance.

Getting People Registered

After you've gotten yourself registered, the next step is registering as many pro-rights voters as you can.

In many states, you can take voting registration sheets and sign up new voters yourself. Once the forms are filled out, you mail them to the county election commission. Be sure to read the instructions carefully, and follow them exactly. One tiny error could easily invalidate a whole sheet of new voters.

In states that don't have registration by mail, you can still distribute how-to-register information, and encourage individuals to register. Lots of potential voters who are intimidated by the bureaucracy will register once you put the how-to information in their hands.

Gun clubs are a good starting point for voter registration. Just as every gun club member should belong to the NRA, every club member should be registered to vote. No excuses.

In states with registration by mail, all it takes is about 20 minutes at a regular club meeting to distribute, fill out, and collect all necessary information for every single club member to register. The following states allow mail registration: Alaska, California, Delaware, Florida (under special circumstances), Hawaii, Iowa, Kentucky, Kansas, Maryland, Minnesota, Missouri, Montana, Nebraska, New Jersey, New York, Ohio, Oregon, Pennsylvania, Tennessee, Texas, Utah, Wisconsin, and West Virginia.

In states which don't allow registration by mail, a gun club meeting can be scheduled during which to march the whole club down to the election commission, and register *en masse*.

Gun shows and gun stores are other good places to distribute registration material. Gun store owners might want to put a registration leaflet in every customer's sack, and gun show operators might want to give such a leaflet to everyone buying an admission ticket.

And when you're handing out the registration material, hand out some other literature on the right to bear arms, and the threat it faces. (Some good sources of free materials include the NRA/ILA Research & Information office, the Second Amendment Foundation, and the Citizens Committee for the Right to Keep and Bear Arms. See chapter 1 for more info.)

14. A Guide to the Legislative Process

"THE BEST ARGUMENT IS THAT WHICH SEEMS MERELY
AN EXPLANATION."   —Dale Carnegie

Organization of the Legislative Body

All state legislatures, as well as the US Congress, are divided into two houses. (Nebraska, with one house, is the lone exception.) The lower house (with a larger number of members, representing smaller districts) is usually called the House of Representatives, or sometimes the Assembly. The upper house, containing fewer members who each represent larger districts, is usually called the Senate.

At the city or county level, these is usually only one legislative body, generally called the City Council, or Board of County Commissioners.

The practice of dividing a legislative body into two houses is called "bicameralism." In order to become law, a bill must pass both houses of the legislature. Bicameralism provides a check on hasty, poorly-written, or emotional legislation. It's no surprise, therefore, that the anti-gun movement is generally much more successful at the city council level than at the state legislature level.

How a Bill Moves Through the Legislature

Upon introduction by a legislator, the bill is assigned a number. The number reflects the house of origin, and the order of introduction. For example, if the bill is the 52d bill introduced in the Senate during the year, the bill will be "S. 52" or "S.B. 52." (The "B." stands for "Bill.")

Once the bill has been introduced and assigned a number, it should be available from the "bill room" of the legislature.

Make sure to notify your National Rifle Association state liaison and the Citizens Committee for the Right to Keep and Bear Arms about any gun-related bills that are introduced as soon as you hear about them. The national pro-rights organizations depend on local activists to be their eyes and ears about gun issues in their area. The national groups have only a limited ability to monitor state legislatures, and almost no ability to monitor city and county government. They need you to keep them up to date.

State legislatures and city councils (but usually not boards of county commissioners) have committees that specialize in particular subjects. A bill dealing with firearms issues will usually be sent to the Judiciary Committee, although there are sometimes other committees, such as Public Safety, State Affairs, Military Affairs, or Local Affairs that might hear the bill.

The committee will schedule a public hearing, where interested persons will have the opportunity to testify. (See chapter 24 for hints on testimony.) The bill may be revised in committee. If the committee votes to approve the bill, the bill is sent to the full house for consideration.

In rare cases, the bill may be sent to another committee. For example, a bill which increases the penalty for unlicensed gun possession might first be sent to the Judiciary Committee, and then the Appropriations Committee. The latter committee would consider the fiscal impact of the extra prison space required by the increased penalty.

The assigning of bills to particular committees is the responsibility of the leaders of the majority party in the house. Usually the leaders have great discretion. If they favor a bill, they will send it to a committee that they expect will approve the bill; and if the leadership doesn't like the bill, they will send the bill to a committee they expect to bury it.

If the bill survives the committee process, it is brought up on the floor of the particular house for a vote. So if the bill was sponsored by a Senator, it would have been sent to the Senate Judiciary Committee. If approved by Senate Judiciary, the bill would be voted on by the full Senate. If approved by the full Senate, the bill would then be sent over the House of Representatives.

Once in the House of Representatives, the bill would go through the same process, being assigned to a committee, and if successful in committee, being voted on the full House of Representatives.

Thus, opponents of a bill have at least four separate opportunities to kill it: once in Senate Committee, once on the Senate floor, once in the House Committee, and once on the House floor. As a result, it's much easier to kill legislation than to pass it. This is exactly as was intended by the framers of the federal and state constitutions, who wished to guard against the proliferation of laws.

At the city or county level, there will be only one legislative body, and there may be no committees. So to be enacted, a bill may need only to receive a single vote of approval. This is one important reason why anti-gun forces have been so much more successful at the local level than the state level. This is also one reason why preemption laws are so important, in order to make sure that laws on crucial issues like gun rights are made only at the state level. (State legislatures can, if they wish to, enact laws "preempting" local laws on a particular subject, in order that legislation on the subject be uniform throughout the state; about 40 states have some form of preemption for gun laws.)

If the bill has passed through the legislature, it is sent to the executive branch (the president, governor, or mayor), for approval. The executive may sign the bill, or veto it. If the bill is vetoed, it may become law anyway, if two-thirds of each legislative body vote to override the veto. (A few legislative bodies, such as the Indiana legislature, can override the veto with a simple majority.)

The above discussion is a general outline that leaves out numerous details and complications. Legislators who are expert in legislative procedure can find numerous ways to revive bills that have been killed, to avoid the committee process, and to accomplish all sorts of other strange results.

How to Get Information About the Law

Most state capitols have a "bill room" or other area where interested citizens can pick up copies of proposed legislation. In some states, the bill room staff can mail a bill to you. You make their life much easier by knowing the bill's number. Staffers for your Congressperson can help you get copies of federal bills, although the process will usually take a while.

Studying the exact language of a bill is very important. Careful review of the bill may save you from making false statements about the bill which your opponents (or your legislator's staffer) will quickly refute. In addition, legislators are more apt to be persuaded by people who can discuss the concrete details of a bill, rather than people who just make generic statements about "gun control."

Careful attention to language is also important because major results can flow from tiny revisions in drafting; just removing the word "or" and replacing it with "and" can turn a reasonable gun law into a highly repressive one.

If you need to refer to existing city (municipal) law, the city hall will have a copy of existing city laws. Law libraries, and some public libraries, will have copies of state and federal laws. Most courthouses will have their own small law library.

Compilations of statutes will usually have a key-word index at the end. If you don't find something under "gun," look under "firearms," "arms" and "weapons."

Bound volumes of statutes are not updated every year to reflect new laws which have been passed. The new laws can be found in the "pocket part" at the back of each volume. Make sure to look in the pocket part before considering your study of a particular law complete. If there has been a change made in the last couple years, the new wording will likely be found in the pocket part, and not the main volume.

How Your Congressperson Gets Information

Legislators suffer from the unhappy dilemma of being starved for information at the same time they are drowning in it.

Congresspeople must live and work in Washington, DC, but have to represent the views of folks in their district. Indeed, staying employed as a Congressperson means keeping the folks at home happy. How can you live in Washington, and at the same time know what the folks in Kalamazoo are thinking?

Many state legislators face a similar problem. They live and work in state capitols such as Albany, but have to represent the views of their district far away in Brooklyn. How to stay in touch?

One obvious way is to read the hometown newspapers. But while newspapers are important sources of information, the concerns of journalists aren't necessarily the concerns of ordinary folks. Yet after a while, legislators tend to confuse newspaper opinion with public opinion. So when the editorial board of your hometown newspaper goes on an anti-gun rampage, your representative starts to think the folks back home are against guns.

Legislators also depend on letters from their district, which is one reason that mail operations are so important to most legislative offices. And legislators also rely on the in-person contacts they have when they go back to the district.

Yet while legislators are desperate for information from the district, their are overwhelmed with information about legislation. Even in the smallest state legislatures, elected officials must make decisions about a bewildering variety of topics every day. Lobbyists try to buttonhole the legislators as they walk from one committee to another; bills hundreds of pages long are introduced on Monday and require a vote on Wednesday; and a torrent of printed matter descends on the legislative office every day.

Knowing the twin conditions of information glut and information starvation faced by the legislators, gear your presentations to cure both problems at once. The most persuasive argument you can present to a legislator is how a bill will affect his own district, and how people at home will react—that cures the legislator's problem of information starvation.

Deliver your arguments in easy to understand, carefully-prepared formats, such as a strong one-page letter, or a well-practiced five minute presentation during an office meeting with the legislator. Instead of just handing him a transcript or a book or a stack of articles, you will have already digested the material for him, and presented it to him in a readily accessible way. That cures his second problem of information overload. (You can still hand him the stack of articles that supports the information in your one-page issue summary; he'll be impressed with your thoroughness, and his aide might actually look at some of the articles.)

15. Letters to Elected Officials

"To sin by silence when they should protest makes cowards out of men."

—Abraham Lincoln

The section on letters is one of the longest in the book. Why? Because writing to legislators and other public officials is the single most effective way for a regular person to influence the political process. In preserving Second Amendment rights, nothing is more important than exercising the First Amendment right to write letters. For ease of reading, we refer to "legislators" in this chapter, but the suggestions are equally applicable to any public official

Style and Mechanics

Include your *return address,* so the elected official can recognize that you're from her district, and can send you a reply.

If know or have met the legislator, and feel it is appropriate to address him/her with a first name, do so. (A familiar salutation will get more attention from the staffer, but will annoy the legislator if you're never really met him.) If you're not in a position to write "Dear Pat," then use either of the following *salutations* for Senators:

Dear Senator

Dear Senator Grobnowski

The salutations for a member of the House of Representatives can be any of the following:

Dear Representative Zortch

Dear Representative

Dear Congressman

Dear Congresswoman

Dear Congressman Fudpucker

Dear Congresswoman Zortch

Dear Mr. Fudpucker

Use the same principles for other officials. "Dear Governor" and "Dear Governor Jameson" are both fine; "Dear Backstabbing Liar" isn't.

Keep the letter to *one page* or less. It's much more effective to use your time to write several short letters instead of one long tome.

If you'd like to convey more information than can fit on one page, send along copies of supportive printed materials, such as newspaper and magazine articles, or other studies.

Type the letter if you can; otherwise *write neatly*.

If you have personal or business *stationary*, use it.

If you know the fax number for the office you're writing to, send a fax, since faxes (being rarer than letters) get noticed.

When you sign the letter, don't bother to include your affiliation with a pro-rights organization (unless you're writing on behalf of the organization). Your legislator already knows what the NRA thinks about the bill, so adding "NRA Life Member" to your signature block doesn't tell the legislator anything new. Gun rights groups get their influence from citizen activists, not the other way around.

In contrast, signing something about your role in the community (college student, bus driver, nurse, or the like), may help the legislator learn about the broad cross-section of the community that is pro-rights.

Originality is essential. You don't have to go do your own statistical analysis of the effectiveness of state waiting period laws. But you do have to say things in your own words. Simply mouthing the slogans from pro-gun sources shows that you didn't care enough to think up your own language. Since you appear less committed, your letter will be less influential.

If you feel shy because you may not write as smoothly as does someone who writes for a gun magazine, don't worry. Legislators aren't looking for superior rhetoric and linguistic excellence. They just want to know that you care.

Originality is also essential in the physical letter. Don't

even think of writing one letter, and sending photocopies to several elected officials. If the issue isn't important enough to you to send an original copy, the legislator won't worry much about pleasing you with his vote.

Of course you can use your word processor to send various original print-outs of the same text to several legislators. As far as the legislators can tell, they're getting an original.

You can save time by keeping a letter-writing file containing the addresses of officials you write to. Chapter 16 of this book contains addresses for many federal officials, and includes space for you to pencil in the addresses of everyone you write to.

Encouraging other pro-gun people to write is an excellent idea. Gun clubs can have "letter parties" at their monthly meetings. Bring a supply of paper, envelopes, and pens, and let the club know about what's going on in the legislature. Fifteen minutes later, all 25 members have written letters that are ready to be stamped and mailed.

When

The time to write a letter is whenever a gun bill is being considered by a legislative body. Over the course of a typical year, everyone ought to write at least two letters each to her US Representative, two Senators, President, Governor, and state legislators. Some hardworking folks will write more often, and as long as they don't write to the same official more than once every month or two, every extra letter helps.

The time to violate the one letter/month letter limit is for the follow-up letters described below.

Who

The most important people to mail to are people whose elections you vote in. A Congressman from California doesn't care a lot about what people in West Virginia think. So when you write people whose election doesn't depend on your vote, focus on people who might want to stay on your good side anyway.

The US Representative who represents a district on the other side of your state may care about you if he's thinking of running statewide for Senator or Governor.

Also, if a Congressperson has taken a leadership role on pro-rights issues, send him or her a thank-you no matter where you live. The Congressperson will like the idea of becoming a nationally-known leader.

Substance

Be polite. Honey catches more flies than vinegar.

A letter should be about *one particular issue* or bill, which the letter should identify right away. If you know the bill number, mention it. For example: "I am writing to let you know of my opposition the proposal to outlaw many semiautomatic firearms, Senate Bill 666."

Offer *reasons* why your action would be a good idea: "The preemption bill would make gun laws uniform throughout the state. Everyone will have an easier time obeying one consistent set of laws, instead of hodgepodge of city and county laws."

Mention anything about *your background* that would be especially interesting to the official. If you are affiliated with law enforcement (e.g., police officer, former prosecutor), say so. Same if you're a kid. (Only people who are presently children should say so; being a former child doesn't count.)

It seems counterintuitive that being under the voting age would make a legislator more interested in your letter, but it's true. First of all, the legislator expects you to become a voter one day. Second, children and teenagers are less involved than are adults in political issues, so the fact that you are involved stands out all the more. Most importantly, children and teenagers get less mail than adults do, and tend to treat the mail they do get as more significant. Thus, the legislator thinks that his letter to a young person may be brought to a history or civics class for discussion, or at the very least talked about within the young person's family.

If you have voted for the elected official before, or

contributed to her campaign, or are an active member of her political party, let her know. Of course *don't* make something up.

If you are familiar with any of the legislator's past acts or words on the gun issue, weave them into the letter. For example, "During your campaign, you stated at a speech at South Bonaparte High School that you were against gun control. I hope you will be able to maintain the pro-rights commitment you made then by voting against the waiting period bill." Or: "Your vote several months ago in favor of the ban on semiautomatic firearms was very disappointing. Too many of our American rights have already been eroded. I hope you will be able to protect what's left of the right to bear arms, and vote against the waiting period bill."

Personalize the letter as much as you can. If you met the legislator ten weeks ago at a public event, say so. It's okay if all the meeting amounted to was you shaking his hand and saying "I'm John Josephson," and all he said was "Nice to meet you."

The prior meeting need not have had any policy discussion to be worth mentioning in your letter: "It was good to say hello to you last month at the county frog-jumping contest. I'd like to let you know about my concern regarding the upcoming vote on S. 228, the handgun waiting period bill."

Likewise, if you've met or talked with a staffer, say so: "I called your office last May to discuss the gun issue, and had the pleasure of talking with your assistant Bob Anderson." And if the staffer was pleasant or helpful, say so.

Things not to do

Getting hysterical about the issue or making excessive assertions doesn't work. "If the gun registration bill is enacted this year, all guns will be confiscated next year, and the Communists will take over the year after that" will not convince anyone.

Bragging about how important or influential you are will not be persuasive. If you're influential, use your influence to convince other folks to write to the legislator.

Follow-through

Less than one percent of people who write to Congress write a response to their Congressperson's reply letter. Moreover, big lobbying organizations have no ability to generate reply letters, so legislators who read a reply know that you are strongly motivated. Accordingly, follow-up letters get noticed by the Congressional staff. And since your follow-up letter probably can't be replied to simply with a form letter, the mail staffer may have to write an individual reply, which will of course engage his attention all the more.

Follow-up to the Evasive Reply

Your follow-up letter needs to be carefully keyed to the legislator's reply. Be on the lookout for replies that were designed to give the impression that the legislator is on your side, but actually made no commitment. Phrases such as "I am happy to let you know that hearings on this issue have been scheduled," "Many people share your concern," "I will keep your views in mind when the bill comes for a vote," or "I am following this legislation carefully," do not, in themselves, indicate anything about the legislator's actual view or intended actions.

If the legislator sent you an evasive reply, write back and *politely* ask for some substance: "Thank you for replying my recent letter about semiautomatic prohibition. Unfortunately, the reply didn't answer the most important question: do you support or oppose the prohibition?" (From here, you can proceed as usual, offering an argument or two in favor of the pro-rights position.)

Follow-up to the Negative Reply

Another type of letter you may get, rather than being evasive, may forthrightly explain that the legislator disagrees with you. In this case, write back, and refute his arguments. However much the stupidity or prejudice displayed by the letter may anger you, don't letter your anger show through in your reply. Remain polite.

Refuting the legislator's arguments can be difficult sometimes, because the legislator is likely getting his "facts" from the anti-gun lobby, and the facts may have no connection to reality. For example, if he tells you that "semi-automatics are 20 times more likely to be used in a crime than other guns," you may have trouble refuting the claim, unless you are happen to know that the "20 times" figure is a distortion of statistics about firearms traces analyzed by Cox newspapers. (For the truth about the "20 times" statistic, see *The "Assault Weapon" Panic*, Issue Paper, discussed in chapter 1.)

So don't worry about refuting every single sentence, if you don't have the facts at hand. Limit your reply to pointing out errors by the legislator for which you do have the facts available.

If any new facts have come to light about the issue, bring them up in the letter, to offer the legislator a chance to reconsider.

Include in the follow-up letter a question or two, designed to force a response from the legislator.

In your reply, recognize that the legislator was at least honest enough to tell you how he feels. Here's a sample follow-up.

Thank you for answering my recent letter about semiautomatic prohibition. I appreciate your honesty in stating that you would support a gun ban. I think however, that your position may be based on some mistaken facts.

For example, your letter claimed "There is no reason why anyone needs a machine gun in today's society." Actually, the semiautomatic prohibition has nothing to do with machine guns. While some semiautomatics look like machine guns, they do not fire like them. A semiautomatic fires only one bullet at a time—just like every other gun. Would you agree that gun laws should be based on how guns actually function, and not how they look?

Two weeks ago, the Hometown Gazette ran a story detailing how so-called "assault weapons" are never used in crime. A copy of the story is enclosed. In light of the new information, perhaps you would want to re-evaluate your position regarding these guns.

Finally, I would like to point out that semi-automatics are very good guns for home defense. Because the operation of the semi-automatic action diverts recoil energy away from the shooter, the gun is easier to fire accurately, and there is less chance of a stray shot. Were you aware that semiautomatics are therefore actually safer for self-defense than other guns?

Follow-up to the Positive Reply

What would you think of a parents who scolded their children when they did something bad, but ignored them when they did something good? Well that's how most Americans treat their legislators. No wonder things are such a mess!

If you've written your legislator to ask to take a pro-rights stand, and he writes back to say he will, by all means send him a thank you letter. Supply some positive reinforcement.

Consider making photocopies of the legislator's positive letter, and giving them to your pro-rights friends. And when you write to thank the legislator, tell him about how you're circulating his letter. In effect, you've multiplied his favorable interaction with one constituent into favorable interactions with a dozen constituents.

In your thank you letter, mention any new facts that validate the legislator's pro-rights stance. Send a copy of a recent editorial or article or letter-to-the-editor that supports the pro-rights position.

And finally, your reply can gently urge the legislator to take a more active role on the issue—such as by cosponsoring a good bill, or speaking up on the floor during debate.

A sample thank you:

Thank you for responding to my letter from last month, and letting me know that you support the firearms preemption bill. You are absolutely right that things will be easier on the police and on ordinary folks if there is one consistent set of gun laws that applies throughout the state.

Enclosed is a letter to the editor from the South Wasquatch Herald. The writer explains how she was arrested for carrying a firearm for protection in East Wasquatch, even though carrying for protection is legal in her hometown of South Wasquatch. The letter is just one more example of why our state needs to have consistent, uniform laws.

In addition to voting for the preemption bill, would you consider adding your name to the list of cosponsors? It's going to be a tough fight to get the bill enacted, and any support you could offer would be very helpful.

Telegrams and Mailgrams

Generally speaking, mailgrams are better than telegrams, because mailgrams contain up to a hundred words, while telegrams are much shorter.

The telegram's sole advantage is that it will arrive within four hours, while a mailgram will arrive early in the morning the day after it is sent.

Mailgrams and telegrams are best when they are not a substitute for a personal letter, but a supplement to it—as a last minute chance to reemphasize your views.

And mailgrams/telegrams do have some value for legislators who still haven't made up their mind at the last minute. As the legislator leaves his office to go to the floor and vote, an aide may tell him "We got 20 mailgrams against the bill this morning."

Who reads the letters?

A major federal official probably won't read your particular letter. But he might. President Johnson would often walk across the street from the White House to the Executive Office Building and personally sample some random letters from citizens. President Johnson, like almost every other elected official, cared a lot about what people thought of him. And he knew that anyone who cared enough to write a letter probably had a pretty strong opinion.

While most Congresspeople don't have time to read every letter, they do take their mail seriously. Most Congresspeople believe that answering letters promptly does more to help their re-election than almost any amount of paid advertising. Letter-writers are people who care about Congress, and are hence likely to vote, and to influence how their friends and family vote.

Congresspeople like getting mail from home so much that if it falls in volume, they get nervous. The issue questionnaires that some Congresspeople send out are intended in part to stimulate mail.

Most state legislators or city councilpersons read everything sent to them. And no matter what, the letter will almost certainly be read by a staff member for the legislator.

These staffers are particularly important people to influence. Usually they are young, well-educated people who are doing legislative mail (and many other staff jobs) for a few years or a few months. Some of them go into politics later, and nearly all of them end up having a reasonably large influence on public policy somehow.

For almost all of them, their job doing letters is the first time that they've worked full-time inside government. They're just learning the ins and outs of a world that's always interested them. They're impressionable, and they beginning to live in a world where big government is regarded more highly than folks in the rest of the country regard it.

At this impressionable time, the staffers are forming their views on issues which they may not have thought about much until then. Gun control will likely be one. When you send letters that are polite and neat and easy to read, and when you use the letters to bring up convincing arguments, the staffers are paying attention.

If you keep up with writing letters several times a year, it's likely that you'll end up provoking some positive thought in a staffer one day. Although you'll never see the exact result of your work, you'll be doing a world of good.

And of course even the staffers who are jaded and don't care still count the mail, and all legislators still pay close attention to the mail count.

Even if your legislator is already solidly pro-rights, letters still help. She can use the letters to help influence her colleagues. For example, if her mail tells her that a proposed federal ban on semiautomatics would harm the many target competition clubs in her district, she can use the fact to urge her fellow representatives to oppose the ban.

Does mail make a difference? Colorado in early 1989 was ready to outlaw all semiautomatic firearms using a detachable magazine. Popular Governor Roy Romer had said so. The major chiefs of police agreed. The President of the State Senate gave the gun ban a special legislative preference. When concerned gun owners tried to hire a professional lobbyist, no-one would accept their money. The lobbyists didn't want to waste time trying to stop a bill that was certain to pass.

A few weeks later, gun prohibition was defeated by a 5-4 vote in the first committee to consider it. Why? Thousands of Colorado gun-owners had written letters to state legislators.

The same story is repeated every legislative season. In 1991, Maryland's anti-gun Governor William Donald Schaefer suffered a humiliating defeat when the Maryland Senate responded to the tens of thousands of Marylanders who sent letters to the Capitol, and rejected Schaefer's ban on semiautomatics.

The pen really is mightier than the sword—or at least mightier than William Donald Schaefer's mouth.

16. Letter and Telephone Master List

"ETERNAL VIGILANCE IS THE PRICE OF LIBERTY."
—unknown, attributed to various notables.

The listings below include blank space for you to fill in information about your own elected officials.

President: 1600 Pennsylvania Avenue, Washington, D.C. 20500. White House opinion line at 202-456-1111.

Vice-President: Same address as the President.

U.S. Senators (two): US Senate, Washington DC 20510. Salutation is: The Honorable (First name and last name). Y o u r Senators also have districts office in your home state; the addresses are listed in the blue pages of the phone book.

U.S. Representative: US House of Representatives, Washington DC 20515. Salutation is: The Honorable (First name and last name). Your US Representative also has a district office in her home state; the address is listed in the blue pages of the phone book.

Capital Switchboard: Will connect you with any Senator's or Representative's office. (202) 224-3121.

Republican National Committee: 310 E. 1st St. SE, Wash., DC 20003. (202) 863-8500. fax: (202) 863-8820.
Democratic National Committee: 430 S. Capitol St. SE, Wash., DC 20003. (202) 863-8000. fax (202) 863-8091

Bureau of Alcohol, Tobacco and Firearms. 1200 Pennsylvania Ave. NW, Wash., DC 20226. (202) 566-7511.

Governor: As a general rule, State legislators and the Governor can be found at the State Capitol. If you don't know who your State Senator and State Representative are, your County Election Commission (also in the blue pages of the phone book) can tell you.

State Senator:

State Representative or State Assemblyman:

Mayor:

City Councilperson or County Commissioner:

Below are phone numbers for state government offices in a few states. Note that the toll-free "800" numbers listed below are usable only with the relevant state.

California
Governor (916) 445-2841.
Assembly Speaker (916) 445-8077.
Senate President Pro Tem (916) 445-8390.
Attorney General (916) 361-3109.
California State Legislature (all Senators and Assemblymen):
        State Capitol, Sacramento, CA 95814.

Colorado
Governor: State Capitol, Denver, CO 80203. (303) 866-2471; (800) 332-1716.
Senators and Representatives: Same address.

Connecticut
Governor (800) 842-2220.
House Democrats (800) 842-8267; 1902.
House Republicans (800) 842-8270; 1423.
Senate Democrats (800) 842-1420.
Senate Republicans (800) 842-1421.

"Turn in Poachers" tip line (800) 842-4357.

Pennsylvania
Governor's Office. 225 Main Capitol Building, Harrisburg, PA
17120. (800) 932-0748.
State Representatives: Pennsylvania House of Representatives,
Harrisburg, PA 17120. (717) 787-2372.
State Senators: Pennsylvania Senate, Harrisburg, PA 17120.
(717) 787-5920.

Texas
Governor's Opinion hotline. (800) 843-5789.

17. Computer Letters

"They'll have to shoot me first to take my gun."
> —Roy Rogers, discussing proposed
> California "handgun freeze."

The advance of technology helps the Second Amendment, as guns get better. Progress also helps the First Amendment, where computers are making writing a letter to Congress even easier than writing by hand or by typewriter. Word processors make it simple to send the same letter to your two Senators, and just change the address. A few months later, the computer letter can be revised slightly, and sent to the US Representative.

Help other people write

If you own a personal computer and a printer, and you're adept at word processing, consider setting up a letter table at a gun show. Visitors to the gun show give you their name and address, which you input into the computer, which outputs letters ready to mail.

At one gun show, a man brought his personal computer and printer, along with pre-written letters to the President, the Republican National Committee Chairman, the Governor, and US and state Senators and Representatives. The man also brought stamps, envelopes, and a good supply of printer paper. He ended up generating 1,608 pro-rights letters, and raised $1212.80 in voluntary donations.

David Bollinger, a Texan who runs a group called "Civil Rights...Civil Responsibility," also sets up a computer for letter writing at gun shows, and offers these tips:

- Make sure to tell the gun show operator that you will need an electrical hook-up.
- Ask a local gun store if they could chip in to pay the table fee (usually 30-80 dollars).

91

- Pull your table about six inches back from the aisle, thereby giving the impression of a small island amidst the sea of customers.

- If you're not charging anything, make sure your display banner says "FREE."

- Bring extra paper, and a large supply of pens, and expect some of the pens to walk off during the course of the day.

- Voluntary donations can be collected in a small-mouthed transparent plastic jug, with a label like "Donations gratefully accepted."

- Bring wire ties with which to control the computer cables.

- A sheet draped over the front of the table helps protect the cables and equipment from children.

- Lay out samples of letters that you will generate. Print plenty in advance, since some will walk off.

- Learn the legislative district boundaries for the areas near the gun show, since many people will not know who their representatives are.

- Morning hours will be slower than the afternoon.

- Don't get mad at people who don't stop at the table to write a letter. They may have already written on their own.

- Do some advance research, and prepare letters tailored to the different officials that people will be writing too. A letter to the President might have a different content than a letter to a pro-gun Representative than a letter to an anti-gun Senator.

- Bring some carts for hauling your equipment in and out of the show.

- Don't have the letters pre-metered, and don't mail them in zip code bundles. The letters make more of an impact if they arrive one at a time, with less of a mass-produced look. (Encouraging people to add a "p.s." can also help individualize the letters; but any letter is much better than no letter at all.)

To make things even easier, Bollinger has written a

computer program called "Letergen" designed especially for use at gun shows. It's not a program suited for a computer novice; a user needs to be familiar with terms such as "ASCII," "path," and "print buffer." The program also requires a few hours of work entering legislators' addresses and draft letters before it's ready to use at a gun show. But once it's up and running, Letergen can help you generate a lot of letters very quickly. The only flaw is that the program's model "anti" letters (chastising legislators for bad votes) are too hostile; happily, the program allows you to write your own model letters. Bollinger sells a DOS version for five dollars. If you want the program, write to David Bollinger at 7410 Silent Sunset, San Antonio, TX 78250, (512) 647-0547. Make sure to specify the disk size and density you want.

18. Petitions

"CONSTITUTIONS ARE CHECKS UPON THE HASTY ACTION OF THE MAJORITY. THEY ARE SELF-IMPOSED RESTRAINTS OF A WHOLE PEOPLE UPON A MAJORITY OF THEM TO SECURE SOBER ACTION AND A RESPECT FOR THE RIGHTS OF THE MINORITY."
—President William Howard Taft, veto of the Arizona Enabling Act, August 22, 1911.

Petitions have played a long and honorable role in the American struggle for freedom. Besides helping to influence government, the gathering of petitions is valuable in its own right, since it stimulates debate and individual involvement. If done correctly, petitions can also stimulate media interest.

Like any other request to a government official, the petition should ask the official to take a particular action.

The message of the petition should be short enough to be easily read in a few seconds by a person who is thinking of signing. The message should be stated directly and forcefully. For example: "We the undersigned residents of Kansas support the right of law-abiding persons to own the type of firearm best-suited to their needs. We urge our representatives to vote against bans on semiautomatic firearms, which have many legitimate uses for personal protection, hunting, and target shooting."

And the message should not contain ideas or references that the average person would not recognize. A petition isn't the place for quotations from the Wright, Rossi, & Daly National Institute of Justice study.

Petitions are good when you have a large mass of enthusiastic volunteers who have little experience. The petition gets the volunteers into action, and creates community outreach and discussion.

When Willie Sutton was asked why he robbed banks, he replied "That's where the money is." To gather petitions, go "where the people is:" colleges, busy downtown sidewalks, factory gates, parks, county fairs, and other similar places.

Remember that private property owners—including shopping mall owners—have a right to exclude you. (A few states, including California, require mall owners to make their space available to the public for political activity.) And on public property, be careful not to obstruct access to buildings, or to impede the flow of pedestrian traffic.

After someone signs the petition, hand him a leaflet, encouraging further action. After all, by signing the petition, he's already indicated that he's friendly. The leaflet might urge him to write or call certain elected officials to voice his support on the issue raised in the petition. The leaflet should supply the names, full address, and telephone number of elected officials.

If you get a large number of petitions, stage some kind of dramatic presentation to their target, and invite the media along. And since you've gone to all the work of gathering the petitions, bring your own photographer along to record the presentation.

Good occasions to present petitions to elected officials are when you meet with the official, or when you testify at a public hearing, or when the official attends a meeting of a pro-rights organization you are affiliated with.

While petitions have value, they are far from the most effective way to influence elected officials. What officials look for in judging public sentiment is depth of commitment. One person who makes the personal effort to write a letter to Congress does more good than 15 people who sign petitions. (Likewise, sending in pre-printed postcards is not a particularly powerful way to get a legislator's attention.)

So in deciding whether to start a petition drive, consider how you want to deploy your resources. If the folks out gathering petitions from the public in general could instead be encouraging other pro-gun folks to write actual letters, the time might be better spent on letter generation. Still, petitions offer an opportunity to interact with the public, and can be a lot of fun.

19. The Magic Words

"NEVER DOUBT THAT A SMALL GROUP OF THOUGHT-
FUL, COMMITTED CITIZENS CAN CHANGE THE WORLD.
INDEED, IT'S THE ONLY THING THAT EVER HAS."
— Margaret Mead.

A few years ago, the book *Everything I Needed to Know I Learned in Kindergarten* came out. The title is particularly appropriate for communications with legislators. Like a kinder-gartner, a legislator may understand virtually nothing of what you're talking about. He may never have touched a gun in his life. And so, as we discussed above, it's important that you explain you point of view to him in a well-organized fashion that doesn't assume a lot of knowledge about the issue.

Also, just like Dave's teachers insisted in kindergarten, the "magic words" of "please" and "Thank you" really do help you get along. Some Congressmen get dozens of letters a week, and others get thousands. But no-one gets more than a handful of thank you letters.

In a sea of pleas asking a Congressperson to do some-thing, a thank you is a pleasant surprise to the Congressional aide reading and responding to the mail.   Another reason thank yous are important: After a pro-gun vote, the legislator stops hearing from the pro-rights forces (who are content with the vote) and starts catching grief from the antis, particularly the antis in the media. A nice thank you letter helps remind the legislator that the pro-rights forces are still there, even after the vote.

Praise need not be limited to perfect legislators. If a legislator has generally been anti-gun, but then casts a pro-gun vote, give him some applause.

Just as being nice helps our cause, being a jerk helps our enemies. Don't call legislators late at night; don't show up at their home unannounced; and don't assume that people who disagree with you have evil motives. Several years ago, the Philadelphia City Council enacted a severe law requiring police permission to buy a handgun; the bill might have been defeated, but a few bad apples ruined our cause by making abusive phone calls to the Councilpersons.

Remember, our objective is to demonstrate that people who own guns are just as responsible (maybe even more so) as anyone else. It's the gun prohibitionists who want legislators to think that gun owners are a bunch of borderline psychopaths, and it's the irresponsible gun owners who assist the gun control lobby.

20. Telephone

"On the 18th of April in Seventy-Five
Nary a man is now alive, who remembers that
famous day and year,
of the midnight ride of Paul Revere"
—Henry Wadsworth Longfellow.

When Paul Revere (and also William Dawes and Samuel Prescott) rode through the night yelling "The British are coming; the British are coming!" they were alerting Americans that the next day, the British redcoats would be marching on Lexington and Concord to seize Americans' arms there.

Because of the heroic rides of Revere and Dawes and Prescott, American militiamen were assembled ready to face the British the next morning on the Lexington Green and on the Concord Bridge.

The Americans were routed at Lexington, but at the Concord Bridge, there "the embattled farmers stood, and fired the shot heard 'round the world." The men of Concord smashed the Redcoats, and chased them all the way back to Boston. The American Revolution had begun and America had won the first battle—all because three brave men had risked their lives to alert their fellow citizens.

Today, it wouldn't be very efficient to jump on a horse and yell "The bureaucrats are coming; the bureaucrats are coming." But they are coming, and they want your guns. Success in a legislative committee hearing, like success in battle, depends on turning out large numbers of well-prepared forces. In mobilizing the pro-rights forces, the telephone today does that work that Paul Revere's horse did in 1775. The phone tree is more comfortable than a midnight horse ride, but it's just as important.

Calling Legislators

Just as powerful as letters are telephone calls. Telephone calls also allow you to fire one last salvo in the final days before a crucial vote. It's always helpful for an undecided legislator to be told by his aide "Thirty calls came in this morning in support of the preemption bill."

Most of the same rules that apply to writing to elected officials apply to phone calls too: stick to a single action you want the official to take (like vote for a particular bill). Express yourself politely.

When you call, ask for the legislator's assistant who deals with right to bear arms issues.

The address and telephone master list in chapter 16 lists the numbers of some elected officials, and provides room for you to add more.

Phone Trees

One of the most effective legislative tactics for gun clubs and local gun rights groups is to set up a phone tree.

The tree operates as a system for one person (such as the Chair) to call five people (or thereabouts) who in turn call five more people, who in turn call five more, until the whole club gets the telephone tree message—hopefully within 24 hours or less. The organizational chart for the telephone tree lists exactly who will call whom, and at what phone number. Persons who can be counted on to be especially responsible (and to call back later if the first call goes unanswered) should be placed near the beginning of the tree.

An alternative to the phone tree is the phone circle. There, the initiator calls person one, who calls person two, who calls person three, until the last person is called. The last person then calls the initiator, who then knows that the circle has been completed, and everyone has been called.

Phone circles are best for groups of a dozen or less people. If the initiator hasn't received his confirmation call on time, he can begin calling through the circle, to see where the circle was broken.

Phone trees are much more effective than phone circles at reaching larger groups of people rapidly. Their weakness is that if one person near the top of the tree neglects to make his calls, a large number of people down the line will never be notified. Thus, the phone tree organizers need to make spot calls, to check the progress of the message down the tree.

Telephone trees are used for rapid mobilization, when there's no time to wait until the next club meeting. Trees can tell members about upcoming legislative hearings, or remind them to vote on election day, or urge them to attend a rally.

The tree message has to be simple, because complicated messages get garbled when passed through several people. The purpose of a tree isn't to educate; it's to mobilize people who are already inclined to our point of view. After all, Paul Revere road through town with a simple message that "The British are coming." He didn't offer detailed arguments about why King George's tax policies were unfair.

The importance of telephone trees is proven every legislative season, when gun club members and their friends and families pack a room to watch a hearing on a bill affecting gun rights. It makes a very powerful impression on legislators when they see the whole room filled with pro-rights citizens.

Phone trees are particularly important at election times. A few dozen votes is often the margin of victory in tight state representative or city council seat. If you and a few friends can make a few hundred phone calls in the two weekends before the election, you can put a pro-gun candidate over the top.

21. Visiting Your Legislators and their Staff

"FREEDOM EXISTS ONLY WHERE PEOPLE TAKE CARE
OF THE GOVERNMENT."   —Woodrow Wilson

How to Set up a Meeting

Ask for one. If you'll be in the capital city, call and ask to make an appointment. Or call the legislator's hometown office, and ask for an appointment when the legislator is in town.

If the legislator just doesn't have room in her schedule, you'll probably be given an appointment with a staff assistant. That's fine too.

Don't take the legislator sending a staff assistant to meet you as a personal snub. Legislators have overwhelming demands on their time. It's nearly impossible to get a meeting with a United States Senator, unless you are from a very small state.

Your chances of getting an appointment with the legislator herself, or of getting a relatively longer meeting with the staffer, increase if you are making the appointment for a group of people. (Seven people is about the largest practical size for an office meeting.)

The comments below refer to meeting with a "legislator," but are equally applicable to other public officials, and to assistants to those officials.

Preparation

Familiarize yourself in detail with the legislator's voting record on the gun issue. Your NRA state liaison or the CCRKBA staff will usually have the legislator's history on file.

Take along a one-page fact sheet, with a concise summary of the issue you want to discuss. Legislators appreciate having arguments boiled down to their essentials, and preparing the fact sheet will help you collect your own thoughts.

As you prepare what you will be saying to the legislator, make sure that you have hard facts to back up every single statement you make.

If you want to bring more material, to give the legislator

as background, bring some editorials or newspaper clippings; write your name and address on the items, so that when the legislator or his staffer reads it later, he'll remember where it came from.

Also remember that legislators are in the business of making laws, just as meat factories are in the business of making sausage. So if you tell a legislator that gun control is not the solution to crime, be prepared to be asked if you have any better solutions.

Similarly, many legislators understand that gun control won't do a lot of good, but they think it might help a little, and they feel a need to "do something." So be prepared to explain how the particular gun control would not only be ineffective, but would be actively harmful.

In addition, legislators want to vote for each other's bills. This is particularly true for legislators of the same party. The desire stems partly from a natural inclination to get along with the people you spend all day with, and partly from the necessity of maintaining friendships to get the legislator's own bills passed. As a result, you need to look for ways to help the legislator protect the Bill of Rights *and* keep on a positive plane with his fellow legislators. For example, a bad bill can often be fixed with some simple amendments. If you suggest to your legislator that he introduce amendments to a bill—rather than just oppose the bill outright—he can amend the bad bill into a good bill, and can stay on good terms with the bill's sponsor.

It's extremely important (and this also applies when you testify before a legislative committee) to read the bill in question thoroughly. Get together all of the pro-rights people who will be attending for a "pre-meeting" to discuss the agenda, and map out who will say what. Designate one person as the group leader, who will lead the meeting through the agenda.

The visit should be confined to one topic, such as a particular piece of legislation. You should present the legislator with concrete acts you would like him to take (such as cosponsoring a bill).

During the Visit

BE ON TIME! In fact, plan to be early, thereby leaving time for getting stuck in traffic, lost, etc. The legislator may run on a very tight schedule, and if you're not ready when he is, your meeting may vanish.

While you should be early, accept the risk that the legislator may be extremely late. He may be coming from another meeting someplace else, and be unavoidably delayed. Take the lateness in stride, and don't let it spoil your attitude for the meeting itself.

Dress in a conservative business suit, or at least a jacket and tie.

Legislators are people too, and appreciate friendly behavior just as much as your neighbors and business colleagues do. So start the meeting with a compliment about something the legislator has done that you liked.

If you know somebody who knows the legislator, drop the name: "Eddie Jackalope, one of your campaign volunteers, said to say hello; we live down the block."

No matter how unhappy the legislator's statements make you, be courteous.

Legislators have to vote on dozens of complex issues every week, and they rarely have time to master a single issue in detail. So gear your presentation to the level of an intelligent generalist—someone who may not know a lot about the gun issue, but who has a good ability to pick out the essential facts necessary for a decision.

Your basic presentation should take a maximum of five minutes. (The entire meeting may be as short as ten minutes, and will almost never be more than half an hour.) The most important points should be brought up first. The presentation should emphasize the impact that the particular issue would have on the community the legislator represents.

Legislators learn how to make decisions in a hurry. Thus, be prepared for direct, challenging questions. Prepare yourself by going over the most difficult questions someone could ask, and coming up with answers.

And if the legislator does start throwing you some hard questions, don't get defensive and assume he's an enemy. Asking tough questions may simply be his way of getting to understand the issue. After all, if he supports you, then he'll have to answer ever tougher questions from his anti-gun colleagues.

In a legislator's office, just like everywhere else, the most successful talkers are the people who are the best listeners. Pay attention to what the legislator is saying, and give his questions the good answers they deserve.

If, instead of talking about the issue at hand, the legislator wanders off the topic of the meeting, bring the topic up again when it's your turn to talk.

If the legislator agrees to take the action you want (cosponsoring a good bill, voting against a bad bill, or whatever), give him the praise he deserves, and let him know that folks in his district appreciate his pro-rights stance.

If you can't tell what the legislator will do, ask him directly. He may tell you that he hasn't made up his mind—which is a reasonable answer. (And it's also an answer that should trigger additional efforts on your part to influence him later—such as doing everything you can to get other pro-rights people to write him letters).

Give the legislator your one-page fact sheet at the end of the meeting. If you give it the legislator earlier, he may focus on the written material, instead of on you.

If you're meeting with the legislator on behalf of a local pro-gun group, ask if you can have a quick black & white photo taken of your group with the legislator. (Bring your own camera, flash, and loaded film.) The picture can be used in the group's newsletter, to demonstrate your good relations with elected officials.

If by the end of the visit you have not met the legislator's aide who deals with gun issues, ask to be introduced.

Afterwards
Send your NRA state liaison a note or give him a call to let him know how the meeting went, and where the legislator stands.

Whether or not you got the result you wanted during the meeting, follow up by sending a thank-you note for the opportunity to have the meeting. If the legislator hasn't taken action one way or the other in regards to your request, ask specific questions about what she plans to do.

This kind of follow-up is very impressive to legislators, because so many concerned citizens *don't* follow up. When you do follow up, the legislator will take you all the more seriously.

Informal Meetings

Formal office meetings aren't the only place you can see your legislators. They're likely to be out and about at all sorts of community events, including fairs, receptions, town meetings, civic group meetings, barbecues, and clambakes. Call the legislator's office, and ask what events she will be attending which are open to the public. Even things which you might think are closed—such as a political fund-raising dinner—are usually open to anyone willing to buy a ticket.

Federal elected officials have an appointments secretary who keeps track of their calendar; state and local officials usually have one assistant who handles that chore and many others. If you call the legislator's office and talk to the appointments person, they can tell you of upcoming times when the legislator will be in your area. In fact, they'll be glad to tell you, since legislators stay in office by meeting and making fast friends with their constituents.

When you know the legislator's next appearance, recruit some friends to go there with you, and give him their own two sentence pro-rights speeches. If the legislator will be at a paid event, such as a political fund-raiser, shell out the money if you can afford it. Besides having the chance for your two-sentence dialogue with the legislator, you can meet lots of other government officials and party volunteers. And when different people at the county fair and the district fund-raiser and the town meeting and the high school talent contest all come up to the legislator and suggest that he support the right to bear arms, he'll get the idea that the gun rights are important to the folks back home.

These informal gatherings are not the place to get the legislator alone for a 15-minute discussion on gun control. But they are a good place to introduce yourself, shake hands, and make an acquaintance.

The legislator will need to circulate at the gathering, and meet as many people as possible, so your opportunity for dialogue may be as little as one sentence or two. Of course the two sentence can be pro-rights sentences, such as "Thanks for all your good work, Mr. Cravath; I hope you'll vote against the waiting period bill when it comes up next month."

Once you're an acquaintance of the legislator, you can write to her on a first name basis, and refer to your previous meeting. (See chapter 15 for the beneficial impact this will have on your letters to the elected official.)

If you're interested in setting up an office meeting to discuss an issue, now's the time to set the stage. When you're introduced, ask "Could I come see you at your office and talk about the waiting period bill?" The legislator will usually say yes, thereby giving you the opportunity to call her office and ask "I met Representative Cahill at Democratic Party dinner last week, and she said to set up a time to come see her and talk about the waiting period bill. What would be the most convenient time for her?"

Even though the representative didn't specifically say so, you may end up meeting with a staff assistant, rather than the legislator herself. As discussed above, that's still good.

22. *Study Your Legislator, Her Friends, and Staff*

"DON'T PUT NO CONSTRICTIONS ON DA PEOPLE.
LEAVE 'EM TA HELL ALONE." —Jimmy Durante.

Every legislator has friends and allies—lots in fact, that's why she won the election. Some of those friends and allies may be pro-rights, and might be willing to put a word in with their legislative friend, if you ask them.

How do you find the legislator's friends? Look in the public record.

Every Congressional candidate, and most state candidates, have to file reports listing their campaign contributors. (Small donations usually don't need to be reported.) The Congressional reports are on file with the Federal Election Commission (FEC) in Washington, DC. (1325 K Street NW, Washington, DC 20463. 800-424-9530.). Reports must usually be filed on a quarterly basis; the quarterly reports are consolidated into a final report for each election. When asking for reports, specify whether you want the quarterly reports, the final report, or both, and the time period you want (e.g., "all quarterly reports for 1983 through 1992.") The FEC charges a photocopying and document retrieval fee.

The state reports will usually be filed with the Secretary of State's office in each state capitol. (At the state level, the position of Secretary of State has nothing to do with US foreign policy; it's mostly a record-keeping job.)

For both federal and state election reports, remember how busy election time is for the agencies that receive and process the reports. If you make a document production request around election time, give the agency plenty of lead time.

The campaign finance reports will list major donations, expenditures, and will also list some of the major campaign officers.

Guides to Congress, such as the *Almanac of American Politics*, *Congressional Directory*, and *Congressional Quarterly Politics in America* all have biographies of Congresspersons.

Available at high-quality bookstores and most libraries, these books tell you facts such as where the Congressperson went to school, what jobs he's held, what religion he believes in, and what issues interest him.

Many state legislatures publish low-cost booklets giving short biographies of the members.

Your town library may also have back issues of the local newspaper on microfilm or microfiche, plus an index to the old newspaper articles. Biographical articles about the legislator will be a strong source of information, and may tell you who his political allies are.

Computer databases such as Prodigy, Compuserve, and Nexis may also be useful. These databases usually contain a specialized political biography library. Even better, they also contain full-text versions of newspaper articles, allowing you to pull up dozens or hundreds of articles dealing with every facet of the legislator's career.

If the legislator is an attorney, his law firm will be listed in the *Martindale Hubbell* law directory. The massive multi-volume reference, available in all law libraries, and some general libraries, lists every attorney or law firm in each state, in alphabetical order by city. For lawyers who are affiliated with large law firms, the directory also often lists major clients of the firm.

As you find out about the legislator's circle of friends, you may recognize some people that you also know. And if you don't know anybody the legislator knows, then somebody in the local gun rights organization may share a common acquaintance with the legislator.

Staff

As we've said, good relationships with staff members are important, so you may want to do some research about the legislator's staff. Detail about the staff person can most likely be found in newspaper articles, and in computer databases which compile newspaper articles.

When you're interacting with legislative staff, a good

staffer will throw the hardest questions he can at you. After all, the legislator is going to ask him hard questions about the staffer's recommendation, and the legislator's colleagues are going to ask the legislator even harder questions.

While the staffer will be trying to ask hard questions, he may ask ignorant ones too. Like the legislator, the staffer must be a jack of all trades, and can't be expected to master every issue. Staffers look good when they provide their boss with solid, reliable information. So when you provide such information to the staffer, you begin to give him a reason to like you.

There are some important differences between staffer and boss. First, only the boss has the authority to make a commitment, so don't demand that the staffer promise you positive action by his boss.

Also, the legislator is used to rough-and-tumble verbal combat. The staffer isn't. (The legislator's facility with human interaction is one reason that she's a legislator, and the staffer is a staffer.) While you don't want to provoke verbal clashes with legislators, you want to be even more careful about keeping things courteous with staff.

Staffers have their advantages too. For instance, they're likely not to be as pressed for time as the legislator is. Your meetings may last longer.

Also, there's a greater chance that the staffer will accept your offers for activities outside the office, such as a gun demonstration at the firing range, or a 25 minute lunch at the capitol cafeteria (Dutch treat).

Likewise, if you give a staffer a pro-rights book or monograph, there's a chance he'll actually look at part of it.

How easy it is to get the staffer's attention is will vary with who the staffer works for. Senior Washington staff for United States Senators are quite powerful, and quite busy.

The above suggestions have focused mainly on legislative assistants—the staff personnel who help legislators evaluate issues and answer mail. Good manners, though, are never out of place no matter who you're dealing with. Smart journalists make a point of being pleasant to the secretaries they meet, since secretaries can be a wonderful source of information about their boss. Making a pleasant acquaintance with everyone in the legislator's office, powerful or not, will make your dealings there more pleasant, and may also, perhaps, yield a valuable advance notice of something important.

23. Help a Pro-rights Candidate

"THOSE WHO EXPECT TO REAP THE BLESSINGS OF
FREEDOM MUST, LIKE MEN, UNDERGO THE FATIGUE
OF SUPPORTING IT."   —Thomas Paine.

Most people have never volunteered for a political
campaign before, and imagine that folks without previous
experience wouldn't fit in. Not at all. The majority of volunteer
tasks are simple and straightforward. Campaign volunteers can
stuff envelopes, or put up yard signs, or make telephone calls,
or pass out literature door-to-door, or hand out information at
gun shows. Enthusiasm and energy, not prior history, is what
makes a good volunteer. Almost any campaign will have a job
that needs doing and which a novice can feel comfortable doing.

The actual jobs you do as a volunteer might have
something to do with guns—such as handing out the candidate's
literature at gun shows. More likely, the volunteer work that
needs doing may have nothing to do with the gun issue. That's
alright. The objective, after all, is to help the pro-rights candidate win, not to spend your time talking about guns.

While the campaign schedule varies from state to state,
the earlier you volunteer, the more good you can do, and the
more chance you have to earn yourself positions of greater and
greater responsibility (if you want them). Also, by getting
involved sooner, you can help a candidate in the primary
election, not just in the general election. Since voter turnout in
the primaries is relatively low, good volunteers can make all the
more difference.

The best candidates to volunteer for are ones whom you
know to be stalwart friends of the Second Amendment. If you're
not sure which race would be the best to get involved in, call
NRA/ILA's state & local affairs office. Ask for the liaison for
your state, and he'll point you in the direction of the most
important local campaigns.

While volunteers make a big difference in statewide
races, they are even more important in smaller, local races, such

as state legislature or city council. The candidates in these races all have less money, and have to rely on volunteers to spread the word.

Besides working as a volunteer, you can:

- Make a monetary contribution to a pro-rights candidate

- Talk to at least 5 friends or neighbors about the importance of voting for pro-rights candidates

- Display a yard sign on bumper sticker for pro-rights candidates

- And of course, vote for pro-rights candidates.

When you're mailing in your contribution, or picking up your yard sign at campaign headquarters, let a campaign staffer know that your support is based on the candidate's positive stand on the right to bear arms.

Does your work make a difference? You bet—sometimes even when we lose. Governor William Schaefer has long been a vehement gun prohibitionist. In 1988, Schaefer's political machine blackmailed regulated businesses like banks and insurance companies to make them contribute to a campaign against small handguns.

Fred Griiser, who led the (losing) fight in 1988 against Schaefer's gun ban, ran against Schaefer in the 1990 Democratic primary. Griiser had only $10,000 to spend against Schaefer's 1.2 million dollar war chest. The press ignored Griiser, refusing to even acknowledge that he was running. Yet in the Democratic primary, Griiser tallied an impressive 23% of the vote.

In the general election, Schaefer outspent his opponent 20 to 1. Schaefer's Republican opponent faced the further handicap of being a political novice who had selected his wife as a running mate. The political pros expected Schaefer to sweep the state and win over 75% of the vote.

But on election day, Schaefer came home with only 60%, and actually lost in a majority of the state's counties. Everyone, including Schaefer's allies, took the relatively narrow margin against a very weak opponent as a personal repudiation of Schaefer's arrogance.

The Governor's opponent, William Shephard, explained that many of his own votes came from Marylanders fed up with Schaefer's support for gun control. Schaefer had long been speculating about a run for the Presidency, speculation which his miserable performance against two weak opponents has now ended.

Recall Elections

Talk of recall elections for legislators who make you mad is almost always political idiocy. The pro-rights vote rarely exceeds five percent, so it's foolish to imagine turning someone out of office in a special election over the gun issue. Wait till the next regular election, when the Second Amendment vote can make a difference in a close race.

Group Involvement

Besides volunteering as an individual, you can join—or lead—election mobilization on behalf of your gun club or grassroots pro-rights group.

Work closely with the candidate's campaign manager, since the manager knows best where scarce resources need to be applied. Moreover, going off on your own jag, without coordinating with the campaign, could backfire, and harm the candidate.

If your group will, in addition to time and toil, also contribute money to the campaign, check out what regulations apply. For example, federal law covers contributions to campaigns for President, US Senate, and US House of Representatives, and imposes some limits on donations by organizations. At the same time, organizations have great freedom to put their money into "independent expenditures." Instead of giving money to a candidate, the organization spends its money on its own advertising or other projects on behalf of the candidate. To check out the rules of play, call the Federal Election Commission's toll-free question service, at 800-424-9530 for any question involving federal election law. For state races, the Secretary of State's office in your capital city will usually have information.

Pro-rights candidates may be interested in doing a mailing to your organization's members. One way to help the candidate is to pay for the postage for the mailing yourself.

In order to preserve your members' privacy, don't give the campaign the actual computer database of your members. Instead, on your own equipment, run a set of adhesive mailing labels for the campaign to use.

One of the most useful things you can do in the months before an election is to publish a voter's guide listing how local elected officials have voted on gun control issues. The voter's guide can also include information about primary and general election dates, and how to register to vote. The NRA and Gun Owners of America both send questionnaires to most candidates, so you may want to work with those organizations, and publicize the ratings they give.

If you compile your own ratings, be extremely careful in recording pro and con votes. *Do not* rely on memory; get official records or newspaper reports for which way the legislator voted. Mistakenly giving a pro-rights legislator only an 80% rating because you made an error about he voted on a bill will infuriate the legislator, and may cost you an ally.

When deciding which candidates to endorse, you might want to invite them to individual endorsement conferences, to meet with you and two or three of the group's most articulate people. These informal conferences can take place at the candidate's headquarters, or a local restaurant, or any other mutually convenient location. The same rules of promptness and preparation that apply for any meeting with elected officials (chapter 21) apply here too.

At the endorsement conference, you'll have the

candidate's attention in a way that you may not have again for quite awhile; right now, he wants your support to help get him elected. The conference can be educational for both you and the candidate.

Offer to write a position paper about the right to bear arms for the candidate. The position paper serves to put in print all those good things the candidate said to you at the endorsement conference; the position paper thereby helps solidify the candidate's commitment, and gives you an anchor to remind him of his pro-gun promises once he gets elected.

In addition, the process of reviewing the draft position paper helps the candidate make up his own mind about the gun issue, and to understand which particular questions involving guns are most important to gun owners.

Write the position paper as an outreach document—with a positive approach that will sound reasonable to voters who don't know much about guns. At the same time, include explicit positions on the topics that are important to you.

Try as hard as you can to endorse candidates of various parties. While the Republican Party is generally perceived as more pro-gun than the Democratic Party, there are plenty of pro-gun Democrats. If your group only endorses Republicans, you may be seen as a captive of the Republicans—and be taken for granted by the Republicans, and ignored by the Democrats.

If both the Republican and Democratic candidates are anti-gun, consider endorsing the Libertarian candidate.

In your first couple or three election cycles, don't feel compelled to get involved in every race. Focus on a few races where your limited resources can have the greatest impact. In general, the smaller the race, the more of a difference a local group can make.

At whatever level you choose to get involved, it is very important that you roll up your sleeves for pro-gun candidates. The US House and the Senate are both closely balanced between pro and anti forces. A couple narrow elections could make the difference between the right to bear arms, and the beginning of the end of civilian gun ownership.

24. Testifying before Legislative Committees

"THOSE WHO WON OUR INDEPENDENCE BY REVOLU-
TION WERE NOT COWARDS. THEY DID NOT FEAR
POLITICAL CHANGE. THEY DID NOT EXALT ORDER AT
THE COST OF LIBERTY." —Supreme Court Justice
Louis Brandeis, *Whitney* v. *California* (1927).

Testifying before a legislative committee is probably
the most dangerous thing a pro-rights activist can do. If you
write letter to a legislator that's not very good, little harm is
done; a bad letter is simply a missed opportunity to do good. In
contrast, a bad witness before a legislative committee can
single-handedly destroy months of effort by thousands of
activists.

Bad testimony is like a tank crew member pulling a
grenade pin—and dropping the grenade in his own tank! The
good guys suffer all the damage. So here are some tips to keep
your testimony from causing friendly fire fatalities.

Should You Testify?

First, find out whether you can or should testify at all. At
all Congressional hearings, and at some state legislative and city
council hearings, there is simply no room for a citizen witness.
The legislators limit testimony to a few pre-selected people.

At other hearings, the committee may only have time to
hear from a half-dozen witnesses (or less) on a particular bill.
And at still other hearings, the committee may take the time to
listen to every citizen who wants to say something.

Before deciding to testify, call NRA headquarters and
talk with your state liaison, or call your state shooting association or other local pro-gun group. They can tell you how the
hearing will be structured, and if the committee can accommo-
date citizen witnesses.

At a hearing where only a few pre-selected people will
be heard, you can still help by showing up with a written
statement (more on that below), and asking the committee clerk

119

to include your statement in the record. The tactic is particularly effective if you can find a friendly legislator who will call attention to it. She might, for example, say, "Mr. Chairman, I would like to enter into the record the written statement of Mr. Fred Goodguy. Mr. Goodguy is strongly opposed to the bill. May his statement be entered into the record?"

If you do testify, remember that there is only one reason to testify: winning. Your objective is to convince a legislative body to take a pro-rights vote, or at least to modify a bill in a pro-rights direction. The purpose of testifying is *not* to get your picture in the paper, nor is the purpose to make yourself happy. Gun-owners who put their egos aside help kill bad legislation. Gun-owners who testify to feed their egos make themselves happy, get their pictures in the paper, and help *pass* bad legislation.

Preparation

Like it or not, *how* you testify may be more important that *what* you testify about. So dress in a business suit. If you don't own one, at least wear a jacket and tie. Women should also dress conservatively.

Whenever you're doing anything that involves dealing with public, including testifying, *never* wear hunting orange or similar paraphernalia. Orange clothes increases the wearer's chances of getting on TV, but mainly because he looks stupid, sort of like the hunter that Johnny Carson portrayed on the "Tonight Show."

Try to arrive at least a half-hour early, so you can get a seat, and coordinate with the rest of the pro-rights folks there. Quite often there will be a local gun rights leader serving as an informal coordinator of the witnesses. If there is such a coordinator, seek him out, introduce yourself, and follow his advice.

When you get to the hearing room, be aware that there is already a waiting period in effect, and it applies to you. Hearings often start late and run overtime. Be ready to wait a long time before it's your turn.

When you're in the audience, waiting for your turn to

testify, be quiet and respectful. Do not call out or say anything rude when opposing witnesses speak. Legislators hate such rudeness, and the press may well make you look like the bad guys.

During Testimony

Be consistently polite and respectful. If a legislator treats you rudely, respond politely. Honey catches more flies than vinegar, and some of the other legislators may appreciate your mature response to their obnoxious colleague. Besides, the legislator may not actually be hostile, but may just be trying to make up her own mind by asking you tough questions.

If you feel yourself getting hot under the collar, take a few seconds for couple deep breaths and drink of water.

Other legislators, rather than being hostile, may strike you as stupid, and keep asking you the same question, thereby indicating that they didn't understand your previous answers. Don't get frustrated. Patiently answer the question again, perhaps with different phrasing. The other legislators in the room will probably understand, even if the one legislator never does.

Address the legislators with appropriate titles, such as "Madame Chairperson" or "Mister Chairman" or "Senator" or "Representative Jones." If you're not sure of what title to use, "Sir" and "Ma'am" work fine.

Remember that the anti-gun lobby thrives on promoting hysteria, and portraying pro-rights citizens as unstable nuts who can't be trusted with guns. Your job when testifying is to defuse the issue, to calm things down, and to demonstrate by your every act that gun-owners are extremely mature and patient. Let the legislators see what good citizens gun owners really are.

Of course a witness can scream at the legislators that they're a bunch of Communist butchers, and he may well get some media attention. Anyone can get his picture in paper for pulling his pants down in public. But such histrionics help the gun prohibitionists.

Even if you are positive that the committee is biased against you, don't attack the committee; you'll simply alienate them further.

In the same vein, lay off personal attacks on other opponents. True, the bureaucrat testifying in favor of gun control may be small-minded enemy of freedom, but now isn't the time to say so. Confine yourself to factual evidence disproving his statements.

If there is a time limit on your testimony, obey it, even if an anti-gun windbag who testified before you ran overtime. Show that our sides plays by the rules.

The time limits that apply to regular folks generally aren't enforced against government officials who are testifying. They can—and do—pontificate as long as they want. Don't waste your energy getting upset about it.

One way to multiply your impact before the committee is to demonstrate that you are speaking on behalf of other ordinary citizens. Maybe you can present the committee with a petition signed by 20 of your friends indicating that they support the same proposal you are testifying to support. Even better, they could write short letters (maybe with your help) for you to offer to the committee. Present the evidence of citizen support with something like "Mister Chairman, before I begin I would like to present you a petition from 25 other residents of Fenario who are unable to attend this hearing, but who wanted to let the Committee know of their strong support for House Bill 649."

Substance

At the very beginning, state who you are, where you're from, who you're representing (if anyone else), and your position on the bill: "Thank Madame Chairwoman for this opportunity to testify. My name is Jack Straw. I live at 2201 Terrapin Lane, in Bailiwick. I am here on behalf of my local community organization, the Southern Bailwick Neighborhood Association. Madame Chairwoman, we strongly support House Bill 2285 for the following reasons."

With a good personal appearance, you've cleared the way for legislators to listen to what you have to say. For substance, the key rule is this: *Be specific.* Quotations from James Madison, or soliloquies about how gun control never works are a waste of time. Most legislators already believe in a general right to bear arms; and the legislators that don't can't be persuaded by rational argument.

What the legislators need is not general philosophy, but specific reasons to vote for or against a particular bill. So if they're hearing a bill about a semiautomatic prohibition, they need to hear about why a semiautomatic ban would be bad. If you're a target shooter, you could explain how you use semis in competition. If you have a semi for home defense, explain why it makes a superior defense gun in many situations. If you're well acquainted with firearms technology, explain how a semi fires at the same rate as a pump action shotgun, not at the same rate as a machine gun. If you're up to speed on gun policy issues, detail how the semiautomatic prohibition in California failed.

Likewise, if you're talking about a gun registration bill, talk about the specifics of registration. Explain how the twenty dollar registration fee would work a hardship on some gun owners. Point to specific examples in other states of how anti-gun police chiefs have twisted registration laws to turn them into gun bans. Let the legislators know about other legislatures which have rejected registration.

Remember that legislators are generalists, not specialists. They may not know the difference between a rifle and a shotgun. They may have no idea of how severe gun control laws already are. (One New York City Councilman thought that guns could be instantly purchased over the counter in his city.) Some of them have never touched a gun in their lives.

So explain yourself in a non-technical straightforward manner that doesn't assume a lot of prior knowledge on your listeners' part.

Anecdotes which illustrate broad points are very useful. If you're opposed to a bill creating a statewide handgun waiting period, tell the committee about how the city-level waiting period in your hometown is administered; while the city law specifies a 5 day wait, the police often take a month to approve gun purchases. You might tell the story of a woman you know who, after her house was burglarized, wanted to buy a handgun in case the burglars came back; but because of the way the waiting period really works, she couldn't pick up her handgun for five weeks.

Make sure that your anecdotes (like everything else you say) can be presented quickly, without extraneous detail, and that you can come to point before the committee gets bored.

Unless you are going to tell a story about something that happened to you, your own personal background should not account for more than a sentence or two.

Name-dropping and similar puffery are *verboten*. The committee will think less of you, not more, if you drop lines like, "I was discussing this bill yesterday with my high school classmate, Mr. Moneybags, who owns three major factories outside of town."

When challenging factual assertions made by previous witnesses or committee members, confine yourself to explaining the truth, without calling the other person a liar. Your factual arguments will be strongest if you can cite a source of evidence: "A few minutes ago, one of the witnesses claimed that semiautomatics are the 'weapon of choice of criminals.' That statement's not entirely accurate. Even in the big high-crime cities such as New York City, or Los Angeles, the police records show that only about 1% of guns seized from criminals are so-called 'assault weapons.'"

Try to avoid repeating points made by previous speakers, unless you've got something new with which to elaborate the point. If by the time the committee gets to you, prior speakers have already said everything you planned to say, it's alright to tell the committee "I support House Bill 2285. The previous witnesses have already made all the points I was going to make, so I'd simply like to ask you to include my written statement in the record, and to enact this important, life-saving legislation."

Visual aids and props, if handling correctly, can be quite effective. In a bill to ban "assault weapons" you could take a picture of an AKS rifle, and a Remington rifle, enlarge the pictures, mount the pictures on stiff cardboard, and explain to the committee that while the two guns look very different, their internal mechanisms and rate of fire are just the same.

Or, you could use your home computer to make a graph showing how gun crime has increased in states with waiting periods. During your oral presentation, you could give the committee members their own copy of the graph, and explain its significance. (When you hand anything to the committee, you will almost always do so by handing multiple copies to the Sergeant-at-Arms, who will then distribute your material to the committee.)

In conclusion, thank the committee for the opportunity to express your position, and quickly summarize the position: "Thank your for the opportunity to testify on the carrying of handguns by licensed, trained citizens. House Bill 2285 will start saving lives and preventing crime the day it is enacted."

Written Statements

If you have time, prepare a written statement to supply to the committee. It's a good way to show you're serious, and will help you prepare your oral remarks.

Bring a clean, typed copy of your testimony for every member on the panel, five extra copies for committee staff, five extra copies for the media, and five more extra copies for unexpected circumstances.

The written statement can go into much more detail than you can cover in the few minutes that you may be allotted for an oral statement. So when making your oral statement, summarize the important points from the written statement. *Don't* read from the written statement. Listening to someone read aloud from a prepared text is boring. You may notice that some of the public officials who spoke before you were reading word-for-word from a prepared text. They're no role model for you; the committee was probably bored with them.

The statement itself should contain your name and address at the top, along with the bill number or topic of the committee hearing. If you're representing a group, the fact should also be noted in the heading. (As we mentioned above, there's no point in mentioning that you represent a gun group. It's more effective if you can arrange to appear on behalf of another organization, such as your church, office, or community organization.)

Other Legislators

Since you've gone to all the work of preparing a good written statement, and driving to the capitol, take the opportunity to garner some influence with other legislators. If your own district's representative isn't on the committee, drop by her office, ask for the legislative assistant who deals with the right to bear arms issue, and give the assistant a copy of your testimony. If you're lucky, the assistant (or maybe even the legislator) may have a couple minutes to chat with you. (See chapter 21, on meetings with legislators and staff.)

Follow up by writing a letter to your home-district representative. Enclose a copy of your testimony ("In case you have any use for a duplicate copy..."). Mention that the witnesses who appeared before the committee overwhelmingly supported the pro-rights position (which will almost always be the case, unless the committee chair decides only to hear from certain witnesses). And offer to supply any additional information the legislator would like help decide about the issue.

Media Attention

If you do testify, consider notifying your hometown media, and providing them with a copy of your statement. If you come from a small town, the local weekly might contemplate doing a couple paragraphs on your testimony in the state capital 200 miles away. Even if the paper doesn't do a brief story on the testimony, having been alerted that local people are interested in the gun rights issue, the paper may pay a little more attention to it in the future.

A media release is only worth doing if you come from a fairly small area. The *New York Times* will not care that you, a resident of Brooklyn, testified before the New York state legislature.

Citizen Hearings

In rare cases, citizens may be entirely shut out of public hearings. For instance, in 1989, the Cleveland City Council passed a semi-auto ban without even publishing the notice of the proposed law on the Council calendar. The Council's deliberate violation of the open meetings law was a conscious tactic to avoid pressure from pro-rights citizens. When citizens are shut out in a blatantly unfair manner, consider holding your own "Citizen Hearings."

Such hearings will be challenging to pull off, and you should therefore work closely with your NRA State Liaison. The hearings work like normal legislative hearings, except that they're run by regular folks, rather than politicians.

Hold the hearings at a friendly forum (such as a Veterans of Foreign Wars meeting hall). Invite sympathetic elected officials or candidates to attend, and to serve on the panel if they wish.

Unlike your governmental counterparts, be fair, and allow all points of view to be expressed by anyone who wants to make a statement.

Inform the media (see chapter 31, press releases), and get as many pro-rights folks to attend as possible.

Hire a court reporter to record and print a transcript of the meeting. Send copies of the full hearing transcript, a one-page summary of the highlights, and a cover letter to all relevant governmental officials. Explain how the official hearing excluded the views of ordinary citizens, and how the Citizen Hearing was designed to let the legislators know how ordinary people feel about the issue.

The meeting is a good chance to mobilize pro-gun people. Collect the names and addresses of attendees on a sign-in sheet, and give attendees leaflets detailing further actions they can take.

PART III

STRENGTH IN NUMBERS:

WORKING WITH THE GUN GROUPS

Every activist should join with fellow activists by participating in pro-rights organizations. At the least, everyone should become a due-paying member of the National Rifle Association. At the most, perhaps you'll become the founder of your own local pro-rights group.

This part of the book goes through the numerous pro-rights groups that would be delighted to have your help, and also offers extensive advice about how to form your own organization.

PART III

STRENGTH IN NUMBERS:

WORKING WITH THE GUN GROUPS

25. Join the National Rifle Association

"AS LIFE IS ACTION AND PASSION, IT IS REQUIRED OF
MAN THAT HE SHOULD SHARE THE PASSION AND
ACTION OF HIS TIME, AT THE PERIL OF BEING JUDGED
NOT TO HAVE LIVED."
— Oliver Wendell Holmes, Jr.

There's a reason that the establishment media says so many vicious things about the National Rifle Association: the NRA works.

The anti-gun lobby desperately hopes you don't join. In fact, Handgun Control, Inc. has begun "Operation Alienate" specifically designed to keep gun owners out of the NRA. The simple act of joining the NRA repudiates Sarah Brady's claim that she, and not the NRA, best represents the opinions of American gunowners.

The best way to join is with a three or five year membership. You get a discount on the annual rate, and NRA doesn't have to spend money sending you renewal notices. Even better, join as a life member. You can spread the payments out in quarterly installments over several years.

Not only does the NRA need your membership, it needs you to recruit other members, including your spouse, children, relatives, hunting buddies, friends who carry for protection, co-workers, and everybody else.

The Georgia State Shooting Association takes a sophisticated approach that other large groups of local activists might consider. The GSSA does computer cross matches of registered voters, handgun carry license holders, hunting license holders, and NRA members. If somebody fits into all of the three first categories, but not the fourth (NRA membership), the GSSA sends a representative to the person's house to politely ask if he or she would like to support their rights by joining the NRA.

New NRA Address

Around November of 1993, the NRA will be moving into new headquarters at 11250 Waples Mill Road, Fairfax,

Virginia 22030. As this book goes to print, no phone number is available. The area code is (703).

The NRA's old headquarters will remain open for at least a year, as a forwarding office. That address is 1600 Rhode Island Ave. NW, Washington, DC 20036. Telephone (202) 828-6000.

Because of the office move, we can't supply you with phone numbers for particular NRA offices, such as the Research and Education division. But if you call the old Washington phone number, they'll be able to give you the new phone numbers as soon as they become available.

26. Support the Second Amendment Foundation

"LET US CONTEMPLATE OUR FOREFATHERS, AND POSTERITY, AND RESOLVE TO MAINTAIN THE RIGHTS BEQUEATHED TO US FROM THE FORMER, FOR THE SAKE OF THE LATTER. THE NECESSITY OF THE TIMES, MORE THAN EVER, CALLS FOR OUR UTMOST CIRCUM- SPECTION, DELIBERATION, FORTITUDE, AND PERSE- VERANCE. LET US REMEMBER THAT 'IF WE SUFFER TAMELY A LAWLESS ATTACK UPON OUR LIBERTY, WE ENCOURAGE IT, AND INVOLVE OTHERS IN OUR DOOM.' IT IS A VERY SERIOUS CONSIDERATION...THAT MIL- LIONS YET UNBORN MAY BE THE MISERABLE SHARERS OF THE EVENT."

—Samuel Adams, speech in Boston, 1771.

The Second Amendment Foundation was founded in 1974 and is dedicated to promoting a better understanding of the constitutional right to keep and bear arms. To that end, the Foundation carries on many educational and legal action pro- grams designed to inform the public about the legal, social and academic aspects of the gun control debate. SAF publishes or distributes over 30 different books and research reports cover- ing all issue related to the Second Amendment and gun control. A full time staff travels the country taking part in meetings, conventions and shows where accurate information about gun rights can be collected and distributed.

The Foundation defends the rights of law-abiding gun owners through legal challenges of anti-gun laws at the local, state and national levels. SAF has taken an active part in cases which have defined the boundaries of gun rights for millions of Americans. SAF retains some of the most respected legal scholars in the nation to write amicus briefs, file lawsuits, and conduct negotiations with state and local lawmakers. The Foundation also took part in the first ever legal symposium on the Second Amendment which brought together America's leading legal scholars on the subject of gun rights and the Constitution.

In an average year, SAF staff members make more than 75 radio and television appearances nationwide. SAF programming is carried on over 160 radio stations on three national radio networks. Public service announcements and advertising are heard by a market of over 100 million people.

In addition, SAF publishes several highly respected periodicals. *Gun Week* newspaper, which has been in existence since 1966, is a weekly publication that provides the most up to date news and information about what is happening to your gun rights across the country. (For more about *Gun Week* see chapter 5.) Since 1989 SAF has also published *Women & Guns* magazine, the only pro-gun magazine written by women, edited by women and designed to reflect women's issues. In September 1991 SAF made *Women & Guns* available on newsstands nationwide.

Membership dues are only $15.00 per year, which entitles you to a SAF membership card, a subscription to the *SAF Reporter* (the Foundation's newsletter), as well as information about the right to keep and bear arms throughout the year. Life membership is $100. SAF is organized under Internal Revenue Code 501(c)(3) and as a result all membership dues and contributions are tax deductible. Contact the Second Amendment Foundation, 12500 NE 10th Place, Bellevue, WA 98005. 1-206-454-7012.

27. Support the Citizens Committee for the Right to Keep and Bear Arms

"TYRANNY, LIKE HELL, IS NOT EASILY CONQUERED:
YET WE HAVE THIS CONSOLATION WITHIN US, THAT
THE HARDER THE CONFLICT, THE MORE GLORIOUS THE
TRIUMPH. WHAT WE OBTAIN TOO CHEAP, WE ESTEEM
TOO LIGHTLY...IT WOULD BE STRANGE INDEED IF SO
CELESTIAL AN ARTICLE AS FREEDOM SHOULD NOT BE
HIGHLY RATED."   —Thomas Paine

Since 1971 the Citizens Committee or the Right to Keep and Bear Arms fought for the Constitutional rights of the American gun owner. Started by ordinary citizens with an extraordinary commitment to preserving the American tradition of lawful firearms ownership, CCRKBA has battled for the gun rights we now enjoy. The premise that an armed populace is more likely to be a free populace is one that goes back to the American founding and has its roots in ancient Greek political philosophy, and still rings true today.

CCRKBA has come a long way in a short time. What was started by a couple a people with a few thousand dollars and a one-room office has grown steadily over the years. Today the CCRKBA has a staff of over 50 people with offices on both coasts and a budget of over $2.5 million. A small group of dedicated individuals has become an organization with over 600,000 members and supporters nationwide.

On Capitol Hill, the Washington, DC public affairs staff works year round with national politicians and pro-gun groups. CCRKBA has initiated or assisted with passage of several of the most important pieces of pro-gun legislation including the Firearm Owners Protection Act. The CCRKBA National Advisory Committee has over 100 elected representatives, authors and statesmen.

The Bellevue, Washington office works full time at coordinating grass-roots lobbying in state legislatures. Satellite offices in other states give the CCRKBA an on-site presence to fight in the trenches where needed. With the help of affiliated local organizations, the Committee has defeated anti-gun legislation in states and localities across the nation. Due to the grassroots orientation of the Committee, a great deal of time is spent informing members of ways they can actively participate in the fight to retain our freedoms.

CCRKBA video and audio presentations have been aired in more than 200 cities. They have been transmitted on numerous cable systems including The Nashville Network, CNN, CBN, USA, and ESPN. CCRKBA also produces literature and other materials on topics related to firearm rights and political action. Staff members travel year-round throughout the country promoting our rights as gun owners. CCRKBA appears at seminars and conferences, schools and guns shows, and on television and radio programs.

Memberships are $15.00 per year, which entitles you to an official membership card, action alerts' which keep you informed on what you can do to stop anti-gun legislation, bumper stickers, access to the Speakers Bureau composed of outstanding pro-gun experts, access to the latest pro-gun books, posters, placards, hats, and other items, and periodic membership surveys that aid in determining CCRKBA policy. Life memberships are available for $150. To join the Citizens Committee for the Right to Keep and Bear Arms write to the Membership Department, CCRKBA, 12500 NE 10th Place, Bellevue, WA 98005 or call 1-206-454-4911.

28. Think Globally, Act Locally

"AND FOR THE SUPPORT OF THIS DECLARATION,
WITH A FIRM RELIANCE ON THE PROTECTION OF
DIVINE PROVIDENCE, WE MUTUALLY PLEDGE TO
EACH OTHER OUR LIVES, OUR FORTUNES, AND OUR
SACRED HONOUR."
—The Declaration of Independence.

When geese fly south for the winter, they adopt a "V" formation. As each bird flaps, he creates an uplift for the bird immediately behind. Consequently, by flying together in a V, the flock gets at least a 71% greater range than if the birds flew individually.

The hardest-working goose is the one at the front of the V, who doesn't get the benefit of an uplift from following anyone. When the lead goose gets tired, he drops back, and lets another goose take the lead.

The principles that work for geese work for people too. Working in a group often helps you achieve much more than you could just by yourself. And when people in a group share hard jobs, everyone remains fresher for the long haul.

Local gun issues affect far more than their locality. If bad gun controls are enacted at the local level, it builds pressure on Congress to make gun control national. As Sarah Brady points out, state and local anti-gun laws are the "building blocks" for severe national controls.

Local groups fight the day-to-day battles on everything from supporting pro-rights legislation in the state legislature to making sure that shooting ranges aren't shut down by zoning laws.

If there's no group in your area, contact one of the existing groups listed below, and find out about setting up a local chapter.

Some of the organizations below have telephone hotlines to keep you up-to-date on developing legislation and other issues.

The addresses and phone numbers listed below are the most recent ones available to us, but some will have undoubtedly changed by the time you read this. Groups are listed by state.

Arizona State Rifle and Pistol Association. PO Box 40962, Mesa, AZ 85274-0962.

FACT—Firearms Action Committee, Tucson, PO Box 27321, Tucson, AZ 85726.

Bay Area Professionals for Firearms Safety and Education. 101 First Street, Suite 131, Los Altos, CA 94022. (408) 865-1720.

Californians Against Corruption. 115 W. California Blvd., Suite 225, Pasadena CA 91105. These folks made a special point of exposing the corrupt record of California Assembly Majority Leader Mike Roos, a notorious anti-gunner and author of the infamous "Roberti-Roos Assault Weapon Ban." After a couple years of pressure, Roos was forced to retire from the Assembly to take a non-elective job in Los Angeles government. Californians Against Corruption now aims its fire at other enemies of the Second Amendment, of whom there are plenty in California.

California Organization for Public Safety (C.O.P.S.). 1451 South Rimpau Ave., Suite 214, Corona, CA 91719. (714) 279-9953. Fax (714) 279-1185. Mr. Mike McNulty. Among COPS many good works has been exposing California government documents which demonstrate that the state's "assault weapon" has been a fraud from its inception; California government officials knew then, and know now, that the guns are almost never used in violent crime.

California Rifle & Pistol Association, Inc. 12062 Valley View St., Suite 107 Garden Grove CA 92645. This is California's NRA affiliate; unlike the NRA affiliates in some other states, the

CRPA is very active in politics, and publishes a lengthy newsletter with legislative updates.

California NRA Office. The NRA is organizing grassroots City Chapters in several California cities. To get involved, call the NRA Grassroots Coordinator, at (916) 446-2455.

Citizens For a Better Stockton, 6333 Pacific Ave., Suite 335, Stockton, CA 95207. (209) 478-9633. Mr. Dale Thurston.

Committee to Enforce the Second Amendment. PO Box 94, Long Beach, CA 90801-0094. Mr. Neil Schulman.

Firearms Education Institute. Box 2193 El Segundo, CA 90245. Mr. Michael Robbins.

Firearms Freedom Society. 7818 Stewart & Gray Road, #209, Downey, CA 90241.

Gun Owners ACTION Committee. 862 Granite Circle, Anaheim, CA 92806. These folks are among the hardest-working activists in all of California. They garnered national publicity in late 1990 by successfully urging Californians to disobey the state's registration law for so-called "assault weapons." Leader T.J. Johnson burned a registration card for the television cameras, just as Vietnam protesters had burned their draft cards. They also do a fine newsletter, *We The People*. Hotline (714) 871-4515.

Gun Owners of California. 3440 Viking Drive, # 106, Sacramento, CA 95827. (916) 361-3109. The GOC is one of the largest and oldest activist groups in California, with 40,000 contributors. They work especially effectively in state legislative races, although they sometimes let other social issues, such as abortion, get in the way of right to bear arms activism.

Quicksilver Coalition. PO Box 28873, San Jose, CA 95159. Mr. Jeff Klopotic.

Firearms Coalition of Colorado. PO Box 1454, Englewood, CO 80150-1454. Hotline: (303) 369-GUNS. A very strong grassroots organization.

Colorado State Shooting Association, PO Box 10425, Colorado Springs, CO 80932. Formerly a sleepy domain of club shooters, now revitalized into an active pro-rights, pro-safety association.

Pro Second Amendment Committee. PO Box 40191, Grand Junction, Colorado 81504. (303) 464-5282.

Coalition of Connecticut Sportsmen, PO Box 2506, CT 06146. (203) 245-8076; fax (203) 245-1957; legislative hotline (203) 722-3030. Publishes the monthly *Hook n' Bullet*.

Delaware State Sportsmen's Association. PO Box 1786, Wilmington, DL 19899.

Unified Sportsmen of Florida, PO Box 6565, Tallahassee, FL 32314. (904) 222-9518. USF's Marion Hammer is perhaps the most outstanding state lobbyist for our cause in all fifty states. Because many trends start in Florida, and because the balance of power in the legislature is never stable, USF's work in Florida keeps us all safer nationally. USF secured passage of the landmark legislation allowing citizens to obtain a permit to carry a concealed weapon for self-defense, after a background check. The trend USF started in Florida is now spreading nationwide.

Georgia State Shooting Association, P.O. Box 93345, Atlanta, GA 30318. Telephone: (404) 874-6805. The group publishes the *GSSA Sentinel*. An effective group in one of the key battleground states.

(Hawaii) **Valley Isle Sport Shooters**. P.O. Box 216, Puunene, HI 96784.

Illinois Informed Gun Owners, PO Box 9116, Downers Grove, IL 60515-9116.

Illinois State Rifle Association, PO Box 27, Kankakee, IL 60901.

Maryland State Rifle and Pistol Association, PO Box 1322, Glen Burnie, MD 21061. Mr. Fred Griiser. An extremely hard-working and powerful state organization.

Maryland Licensed Firearms Dealers Association, Inc., 2201 Victor Court, Silver Spring, MD 20906. (301) 942-3329; fax (301) 942-7946. Many gun dealers in Maryland—unlike their counterparts in some other states—understand that unless they get actively involved in public affairs, their business will be constricted and regulated until it dies.

Gun Owners Action League of Massachusetts. 14 Main St., Box 272, Southboro, MA 01772. (508) 481-5112. How is it that in Massachusetts, where three-term Governor Dukakis supported gun prohibition, not a single major new statewide gun law has been enacted since 1976? The Gun Owners Action League worked harder to preserve freedom than Dukakis did to restrict freedom. GOAL makes a major effort to encourage gun owners to register to vote, a strategy which should be imitated by pro-rights groups in other states. The group makes available to its members a Massachusetts legislative directory, providing phone numbers and addresses for the whole state legislature. (Another good idea for other groups to imitate.) GOAL also runs the GOAL Foundation, which promotes firearms safety, and to which you can make tax deductible contributions.

Motor City Sportsman's Association. PO Box 21383 Detroit MI 48221. Motor City's feisty General Laney has been one of Michigan's longest-standing supporters of civil rights.

Gun Owners Civil Rights Alliance of Minnesota. PO Box 131254, St. Paul, MN 55113. (612) 293-1269.

Minnesota Committee for the Right to Keep and Bear Arms. 4890 Hanson Road, Shoreview, MN 55126.

Western Missouri Shooters' Alliance. 2900 Bedford Court, Blue Springs, MO 64015. Also, PO Box 11144, Kansas City, MO 64119. Hotline: (816) 444-0228. Answering machines/phone lines (816) 229-5920, (816) 597-3533, (314) 567-2081, (314) 434-7322. Very involved in political action, this group publishes a good monthly newsletter, *The Bullet*. The Alliance is a key leader in the fight for laws allowing licensed, trained citizens to carry concealed firearms.

Missouri Citizens for Civil Liberties. PO Box 9140, Richmond Heights, MO 63117. Mr. John Ross.

Gun Owners of New Hampshire, RFD #1 Box 517, Andover, NH 03216. (603) 225-4664. A hard-working group which, thanks to its influence in the New Hampshire presidential primary, has a major national impact. Publishes the monthly *Firearms and Freedom*.

Coalition of New Jersey Sportsmen. PO Box 423, Oakhurst NJ 07753. (201) 389-3355; (908) 889-5931. Ms. Barbara Nappan. Thanks to Governor Jim Florio's plans to confiscate semi-automatics, New Jersey went from the state with the weakest pro-rights movement to the strongest. During the 1991 legislative elections, the Coalition played a major role in ousting scores of anti-rights legislators.

Association of New Jersey Rifle and Pistol Clubs. P.O. Box 66, Highland Lakes, NJ 07422. (201) 764-2433; (201) 661-0634. Like the Coalition of New Jersey Sportsmen, these folks are very involved in turning New Jersey around.

Citizens for Responsible Gun Ownership. Akron, OH. (216) 773-5701. Mr. Ken Zeigler.

Firearms Fact Committee. Cincinnati, OH. (513) 474-6958. Mr. Bob Eickelberger.

Land of Legend Rifle & Pistol Club. Newark, OH. Mr. & Mrs. Bob & Kathryn Dennis. (614) 345-2860.

Lorain County Firearms Defense Association. (216) 327-6655. Mr. Chris Crobaugh.

Miami Valley Association for Responsible Legislation. Dayton, OH. (513) 294-6623. Mr. Mike Chaves.

Ohio Constitution Defense Council. 12900 Triskett Road, Cleveland, OH 44111. Publishes the quarterly *Liberty Bell*. Umbrella organization for the local Ohio groups.

Ohio Rifle & Pistol Association. (513) 293-6194. Mr. Frank Fecke.

People's Rights Organization, PO Box 2652, Columbus, OH 43216; 614-268-0122. Dues $12. An effective grassroots organization, with the common sense to realize that an assault on any part on the Bill of Rights is an assault on all of it.

Citizens Safety Committee, Multnomah County. PO 19448 Portland, OR 97219. (503) 283-4368.

Pennsylvania NRA office. 301 South Allen St., #103, State College, PA 16801. (814) 234-2222. Mr. Alan Krug.

Keystone Second Amendment Association. PO Box 361, Curwensville, PA 16833. (814) 236 1013. Mr. Don Boal. One of the most informative monthly newsletters published by any local group, chock full of interesting information, and marred only by a sometimes overly strident attitude.

Americans Against Gun Control. PO Box 1564, Rapid City, SD 57709. Mr. Bill Wells

Texas State Rifle Association, Texas State Rifle Association, PO Box 710549, Dallas, TX 75731. (800) 876-8772 and (512) 288-6608. Fax (512) 288-1008. Legislative hotline (512) 288-3242. The TSRA is the local branch of the NRA. This hardworking group has its hands full with all the anti-gun laws being proposed in the Texas legislature. They've been publishing the *TSRA Sportsman* for over 20 years. The group also offers TSRA Long Distance, a TSRA Mastercard, and dental insurance. (Other groups take note!)

North Texas Arms Rights Coalition (NTARC). POB 28186 Dallas, TX 75228-0186. (214) 270-4068. Mr. Wayne Burnham.

Wisconsin Pro-Gun Movement, PO Box 51, Hales Corners, WI 53130. (414) 425-5577 phone/fax.

Wyoming Arms Rights Coalition. PO Box 2571, Gillette, WY 82717-2571

29. *Other National Groups*

"LIBERTY DOES NOT CONSIST IN MERE GENERAL
DECLARATION OF THE RIGHTS OF MEN. IT CONSISTS IN
THE TRANSLATION OF THOSE DECLARATIONS INTO
DEFINITE ACTION."   —Woodrow Wilson,
speech, Philadelphia, July 4, 1914.

We've already told you to join a whole bunch of
organizations. Here are some more national groups that do good
work:

American Pistol and Rifle Association. Box USA, Benton,
TN 37307. (514) 644-0440. Mr. Ron Boylan.

Firearms Coalition, PO Box 6537, Silver Spring MD 20906.
This is outfit is run by Neal Knox, one of the most important pro-
gun leaders in American history. A former national shooting
champion, Neal enjoys a keen understanding of not only the
politics of gun control, but also the pleasures of shooting.

As head of the Firearms Coalition, Knox does yeoman
work for gun rights. He authors excellent columns for *Guns &
Ammo, Shotgun News*, and other publications. He also does
extensive lobbying. Like CCRKBA's lobbyist John Snyder, he
is particularly effective at keeping the pro-gun stalwarts ener-
gized and unified. He runs an excellent telephone hotline
providing constant updates on the battles in Washington and
across the country (301-871-3006).

In 1990 and 1991, Neal led insurgent slates of candidates for NRA Board of Directors. Most of Neal's slate,
including Neal himself, were elected, providing the NRA Board
with the most pro-rights composition it has had in years.

Unlike some avid shootists, Neal understands that the
assault on "bad" guns like small handguns or semiautomatics
with plastic stocks is only a warm-up for the assault on all guns.

Gun Owners of America. 8001 Forbes Place, Suite 102,

Springfield, VA 22151. (703) 321-8585. Fax (703) 321-8408. GOA is the third-largest national pro-gun lobby, after NRA/ILA and the Citizens Committee for the Right to Keep and Bear Arms. GOA generally takes an uncompromising stance on gun questions. While the hard-line stance can sometimes cause problems, GOA provided a clear voice on behalf of the Second Amendment in early 1989, when GOA President Larry Pratt, on behalf of GOA's 100,000 members, spoke out immediately and forcefully against restrictions on semiautomatic firearms.

International Paintball Players Association. PO Box 90051, Los Angeles CA 90009. What does paintball have to do with firearms? Well, learning how to run around the woods, avoid the enemy, and shoot accurately under pressure sounds an awful lot like voluntary militia training. That's one reason why anti-gun bureaucrats are determined to clamp down on paintball. In New Jersey, the Attorney General even tried to force people to get firearms licenses in order to buy a paint gun. (It takes about four months to get a firearms license in New Jersey.) The IPPA is headed by attorney Jessica Sparks, a persuasive advocate for our cause. Like many paintballers, she started out with no interest in the Second Amendment; but after playing paintball for a while, she started to recognize the importance of the right to bear arms.

Jews for the Preservation of Firearms Ownership. (JPFO). Mr. Aaron Zelman. 2872 S. Wentworth Ave., Milwaukee, WI 53207. JPFO's membership magazine *Maccabee* is one the most interesting publications of the smaller gun rights groups. Among JPFO's many interesting publications are interviews with a survivor of the Nazi extermination camps and with Armenian victims of Turkish genocide, who explain how gun control helped the killers achieve their objectives. The JPFO initials are appropriately evocative of the JFO initials of the Jewish Fighting Organization which led the revolt against the Nazis in the Warsaw ghetto during World War II. (For information about their book *Gun Control: Gateway to Tyranny*, see chapter 1.)

Law Enforcement Alliance of America. Suite 421, 7700 Leesburg Pike, Falls Church, VA 22043-2618. (703) 847-COPS. As more and more big-city police chiefs push for gun control and gun prohibition, more and more rank-and-file officers are fighting back. LEAA is a national organization of police officers (civilians may also join) which pushes for stronger laws aimed at criminals, and opposes restrictions on the freedom of law-abiding citizens to own firearms.

National Firearms Association, PO Box 160038, Austin, TX 78716-0038. The nation's major association for automatic firearms collectors.

National Foundation for Firearms Education, 440 Park Ave. South, NY, NY 10016. Former head of Amnesty International USA Mark Benneson runs this one. They focus on publicizing writing by folks like Jim Wright and Paxton Quigley.

We Are Aware (Armed Women Against Rape and Endangerment), PO Box 255, Maynard, MA 01754. This organization promotes self-defense by women, and strongly supports a woman's right to choose to own and carry a gun or Cap-Stun. They publish a quarterly newsletter.

30. Start Your Own Group

"DISPERSE YOU REBELS; DAMN YOU, THROW DOWN
YOUR ARMS AND DISPERSE."
—British Major John Pitcairn's futile order to
the American patriots at Lexington, April 19,
1775.

Starting a pro-rights group can be a wonderful experience; you'll work hard, succeed sometimes, fail other times, and do your country a tremendous service. But before you leap, it's important to take a hard look, and realistically analyze what you want to do and what you can do. Assess yourself, and whether you're ready to put the time and emotional commitment into starting the group from scratch. While organizing the group may be somewhat easier than founding your own small business (you won't starve if the group flounders), you will face many of the same enormous challenges.

You must be prepared to handle the virtual certainty of failure. Not the failure of the group as a whole, since it's likely that the group will succeed, and will do some worthwhile projects. But along the way, it is inevitable that you will run into blind alleys, misguided projects, and more snafus than you imagined could happen at once. Any human enterprise—especially one involving a lot of humans—is bound to encounter all sorts of unexpected disasters. When setbacks happen, take them in stride, learn from experience, and move on. If you're not comfortable with taking chances and failing some of the time, then you won't be able to create the opportunities to take chances and succeed other times.

Realistically assess how much time you can put into the organization month after month.

Set moderate goals you can reach. It's like an exercise program. If you start off intent to do a 200 pushups a day, you may not meet the goal, and may give up from discouragement. But if you start with 20 a day, and when 20 become easy you do 30 a day, and so on, then after a while, you may be doing 300 pushups one-handed!

Finally, be professional. Remember the importance of first impressions. Dress neatly. Keep your appointments, start meetings on time, mail out literature when you say you will.

In building a group, follow-up is essential. Send thank you notes, keep a list of names, addresses, and phone numbers of interested people, and invite them to meetings. If a member puts in extraordinary effort, let Alan know, and he'll send your member a certificate of appreciation.

Name

In general, it's better to be for something than against. So consider a name that emphasizes what you're for (freedom) rather than what you're against (gun control). Look at the list of local organizations (chapter 28) for some examples of positive, upbeat names.

Meetings

Unless meetings are held in your own home, book your meeting rooms at least four weeks ahead of time. A few days before the meeting, call to reconfirm your reservation. If you always have meetings at the same time and place ("2d Sunday of every month, at 7:30 p.m."), then it's easier for people to remember to attend.

Gun clubs, apartment party rooms, libraries, schools, community recreation centers, and churches are all good choices for a meeting site. A private room in a restaurant is also possible, but any unless the prices are very modest, some potential members may not attend because their budgets are tight.

In many urban areas, people don't want to drive all the way back downtown for an evening meeting. So have the meeting at a convenient suburban location in an area where you have a lot of active members.

It's true that the members who live in suburbs on the other side of town will have to drive even further than they would to a downtown meeting. But if they were willing to drive downtown, they'll probably be willing to drive ten minutes further. And in the suburb that's hosting the meeting, you may get several more attendees who wouldn't have showed up for something a long distance away.

When the group is starting out (and this goes for booking rooms for speeches too), get a room slightly *smaller* than you expect to need. Fifteen people who show up in a room that can set a hundred may feel that there aren't enough other people to make group participation viable; fifteen people in a room built for twelve will feel that the energy in the group is growing by leaps and bounds.

The small rooms rule, like all the other rules in this book, is not an absolute. If you're having a strategy meeting with ten key volunteers, get a room that holds ten people, not seven.

Show up early for meetings, and make sure that everything is in working order. If the meeting is in your home, serve light refreshments.

Have plenty of free literature (see chapter 1) on hand.

Supply name tags for meetings, and make sure to greet newcomers with a handshake and a sincere smile. Introduce new people to the veterans (or have everybody introduce themselves). Do everything you can to make everybody feel comfortable.

When recruiting new members, remember that high school and college students (whose minds are still open), middle to upper income people aged 30 to 50 (who are generally pro-rights), and small businessmen (who know the perils of excessive government) are often especially interested in pro-rights issues.

At the meeting, pass around a sign-in list for people's names, address, and phone number. Before the next meeting, call through the list, reminding people about the date, time, and location of the next meeting, and inviting them to attend. The calling can be time-consuming, but the personal touch really does make a difference.

When the meeting is finished, ask people what they liked and didn't like, and ask one-on-one for suggestions for future meeting topics.

And lastly, if the group is productive, but the meetings aren't, stop holding meetings, and put the energy that you were using to organize meetings into other projects for the group.

Committees

An effective grassroots group may simply be three people. Such a small group has little need for formal structure; it just needs to get each member going on projects for which the particular member is suited.

Larger groups, though, may need more structure. One effective way to build structure is through committees. A committee consists of a chair—chosen for her reliability and ability to get things done—and as many committee members are necessary. Committees focus on one particular area of responsibility. Some of the committees your group might use are:

- Communications Committee. Works on newsletters for members and other interested people. Informs members of actions by the organization. Coordinates letter-writing campaigns to elected officials. Runs the phone tree/phone circle (see chapter 20).

- Logistics Committee. Organizes meeting times and places, and informs members of upcoming meetings. Also keeps close watch on the legislative calendars of relevant local governments, and informs members about local government meetings involving gun issues.

- Finance Committee. Raises funds for the organization. In addition to soliciting the membership, and raising funds at gun shows, the committee can also ask for help from sympathetic local businesses, such as gun stores. Fundraising is generally more successful when donors know that the money will be used for a specific project, or will have a clear tangible value. For example, next to the donation can at your information table write out: "$15 will pay for printing for one thousand educational flyers."

Press Committee. Drafts news releases, keeps a list of addresses for local media, calls and writes media to inform them of upcoming events. Some Press Committee tips are offered later in this chapter.

The organizational structure above is just an outline. Don't feel constrained to stick with it if another type of committee organization would work best for your group. Each group's organization should be flexible, to reflect the particular abilities of its members.

Membership Lists

Speaking of lists, your organization will likely end up compiling a list of people in the area who are interested in gun rights. Some people who sign up will feel very strongly about not being put in a database someplace, or having their name given out. Respect their wishes.

Recruiting New Members

Emphasize benefits, not features. If you've got a table at a gun show, and are trying to raise individual contributions, point out how your group can benefit the donor (e.g., "we're working to defeat the semiautomatic ban that the anti-gun lobbies are pushing in the legislature"). Don't emphasize features, which may not interest your donor (e.g., "our group was founded in 1990").

At legislative hearings and other gatherings related to gun control, circulate a sign-up sheet in the audience, asking for names, addresses, and phone numbers of people who would like to work together to fight gun control.

Because you'll be operating on a financial shoestring, every source of revenue will be important, and no revenue source will be as important as memberships. Set the dues high enough to cover your cost of recruiting, and to leave something extra for your operating expenses. Twenty or twenty-five dollars would be about right.

Do not prorate your dues for what part of the year they

come in. If your annual dues are $20, don't in July sell a ten dollar membership that expires at the end of the year. Instead, make memberships good for one full year. If it's much easier administratively for you to have all memberships expire at the end of the year, offer people who sign up late in the year some kind of premium, but still collect the full dues amount. (E.g., in July, sell a $20 membership that expires in December, and throw in a free t-shirt as a bonus.)

Consider selling multiyear memberships at a discount. The multiyear memberships are helpful because you don't have to worry about renewal, don't have to spend any resources encouraging renewal, and you get a good sum of cash right up front. So if annual dues are $25, then offer a two-year membership for $40. You'll probably need to be around for a couple years before people are willing to invest in three or five year memberships.

Membership Cards and Paraphernalia

People liking having some tangible token of their membership. During your organization's first six months, new members can have the added distinction of being "charter members," a fact which the membership card should recognize.

If you know someone who can volunteer some graphic design services, ask them to create an attractive logo for your group. And think up a good slogan that the group can put on its membership cards, newsletter, and other materials.

Besides membership cards, you may also want to create t-shirts, bumper stickers, buttons, and similar accessories. Members will enjoy wearing them; non-members will enjoy buying them, and everybody who has one will be a walking advertisement for the group.

Before selling anything, check with your city, county, or state Department of Revenue (or Tax Bureau), and find out the rules regarding sales tax.

For these products—and for everything else you do—it's best to take things one step at a time. Instead of ordering 500 t-shirts, order 20, and see how they sell, see how well the supplier meets your needs, and see if it's a small project that shows potential for becoming a larger project, or if it was an experiment that should be abandoned for more productive endeavors.

If plan to do a mailing to recruit new members, it's conventional wisdom in the direct mail business that self-addressed envelopes more than pay for themselves. If you make it easy for people to mail you money, they're more likely to do so.

In the long run, the cheapest self-addressed envelopes are the Business Reply Mail type. The Post Office charges a you premium to deliver these. But since you only pay for the envelopes that people actually send back to you, the cost savings can be substantial. Check with your local Post Office for the detailed requirements for using Business Reply Mail.

You don't have to get stationary or business cards right away, but when you do so, make sure they look professional.

Personal Skills

Here's the most important tip: *Listen more than you talk.* People will help your pro-rights efforts for their reasons, not for your reasons. Listen carefully to what interests them, and then suggest how your group is supporting their interests. *Emphasize areas of agreement, rather than disagreement.* If you're leafleting a shopping mall, and somebody takes your literature, and says "I think that people need guns for protection, but I don't see what's wrong with a waiting period," you don't need to engage him in a debate about waiting periods. Instead, talk about how your group is working to promote the right to have guns for self-protection (such as by supporting a concealed carry bill, or by opposing gun prohibitions). It's more important to win allies than to win debates, so save your arguments for another day.

In discussions among your group, and in everything you do with the group, don't act like the great dictator. The more you encourage other people to talk and to make decisions, the more involved they'll want to be.

Unskilled as your volunteers may be, they won't stay volunteers long if you just put them at a desk and make them stuff envelopes. The really tedious work should be shared by everyone (especially you) in "work party" atmosphere, with ample beer and refreshments on hand.

And while you're encouraging people to work hard, make things fun. Consider what we know about life in the military: People join the military for many reasons, including ideological reasons and patriotism. But when soldiers are running across open fields under hostile fire, or sleeping in foxholes, their motivation doesn't have much to do with ideology. The soldiers who perform the best in combat are those who are part of a cohesive unit. When you're under fire, your desire to save your buddy's life by pulling him out of a ditch is a lot more important at motivating action than your attitude towards the Bill of Rights.

Similarly (sort of), volunteers will come to your organization because of their ideological support for freedom. But the most important factor in determining whether they will develop into long-term, active volunteers is whether they form friendships with other folks in the group.

Accordingly, make sure that your meetings have plenty of opportunity for socializing. Just asking people to drive downtown, listen to a speech, and then leave, isn't going to promote camaraderie. Having a cocktail hour before the meeting, or beer and pretzels afterward, or making the meeting itself a potluck supper are among the ways to promote conversation. You can also have parties without a formal meeting, and urge members to bring friends and family.

People thrive on praise and recognition, so distribute them out generously. If people take on projects, give them a title. The woman who volunteers to write the press release can become the Media Relations Director, and the guy who drops off the press release at all 15 radio stations can be the Assistant Media Director. These titles aren't meant to be grandiose, but to reflect the training you'll be giving, to help people build skills, and take on more and more responsibility themselves.

In fact, *your most important contribution as a leader will be to help other people develop the skills and confidence to take on responsibility and leadership themselves.*

When big projects are completed, hand out the praise and recognition for those who helped. If you're holding a press conference, early in your remarks thank by name the volunteers who made it happen.

Advisory Council

A group's credibility is enhanced if it has the support of well-known civic leaders. If there are some local elected officials, university professors, business leaders, religious leaders, or similar folks who would support your group's pro-rights objectives, invite them to serve on the group's Advisory Council. Your letterhead can include a list of Advisory Council members.

And what does the Advisory Council actually do? First of all, you should turn to it for advice. The reason that your Advisory Council members have become prominent in the community is that they're good at something. Take advantage of their experience. (You don't need to call the Council together as a formal body; a telephone call to a particular Council member will be fine.)

Perhaps over time, the Advisory Council members will grow even more enthusiastic about the pro-rights cause, and be interested in taking a more active role. Council members might serve as spokespersons for the group, or help with fundraising.

As always, be flexible, and adapt our suggestions to your particular circumstances. For example, if two State Senators—but nobody else—volunteer to serve as advisors to your group, you don't really have enough people to create an "Advisory Council." So make the two Senators "Honorary Chairpersons" of the group. The Senators might even be so pleased with their lofty title that they'd help you send out a press release announcing their new role.

Affiliations with Larger Groups

Affiliation doesn't mean that you simply become a local chapter of the national group. Rather, your independent local group maintains a link with national group, in order that the two groups can share information and expertise

Affiliating with a national pro-rights organization can give you a tremendous leg up in learning the basics of organizing activists. You can benefit from the national organization's years of experience, and avoid learning the hard way about mistakes other activists have made. The Citizens' Committee for the Right to Keep and Bear Arms (Alan's group) is particularly eager to work with local activists.

National groups are also likely to have campaigns in progress that you can join.

New Chapters?

Inspired by your success, activists in other cities may ask if they can form area chapters of your group. If you feel comfortable with them, sign them up. But in the long run (or maybe even the short run), your goal should be for them to form their own group. To help them, offer to share all the expertise and resources you have to get them get started.

Two groups in different cities can still coordinate their activities, but each group will get more done if its energy is concentrated in actual work, rather than in managing a multicity structure.

Newsletter

Once a group gets established, it's a good idea to publish a newsletter. Once a month is a common interval. The newsletter can be as simple as an 8 1/2 x 11 inch flyer, or much more elaborate. Newsletters are great to hand out at gun shows; they help bring in new members, and help alert everyone about projects, elections, and legislative issues.

Newsletters need not look like 4-color glossy corporate reports, but neither should their look like they were produced on a mimeograph machine that saw its best days during the

Eisenhower administration. With today's advances in computers and desktop publishing, it's not to hard to put together a nice-looking newsletter that conveys the sense of organization and efficiency that will attract new members.

The title should be closely linked to the name of your group. If your group is the "East Orange Public Safety Association," call the newsletter the "East Orange Public Safety Association Newsletter." True, it would be more glamorous to call the newsletter "The Liberator," but since you're trying to build name recognition for your group, you need to make it very easy for people (even people who aren't careful readers) to associate the newsletter with the group.

Every newsletter should include a blank form for new members to fill out in order to join. The blank form can ask people which areas they would be most interested in helping in:

"Please check all of the following which interest you:
___Handing out leaflets or manning tables at gun shows
___Making phone calls to voters in support of pro-gun candidates
___Putting up yard signs for pro-gun candidates
___Having a sign in your own yard."

Every newsletter should list the names, addresses, and phone numbers of your two US Senators, the US Representatives in your area, and other public officials to whom you are encouraging people to write. And every newsletter should encourage people to take specific actions (writing a letter, registering to vote, etc.) in whatever battle is going on at the moment.

If the newsletter will be mailed, make it a self-mailer. One side of a folded sheet of the newsletter contains space for the addressee, thereby obviating the need for a separate envelope.

The news that goes in your newsletter can include updates on events in Washington, DC and your state capital, details of your group' s recent meetings and activities, local news relating to the gun issue, facts about guns and gun control, reprints of pertinent material from other publications (telephone to get permission first), and announcements of forthcoming shooting events.

And don't neglect to tell folks what the anti-gun people are up to. Most gunowners are like the militia members of the American War for Independence. When the threat is close at hand, they'll fight with vigor and determination. But when trouble seems far away, they don't take much interest in public affairs. And since the mainstream media doesn't always slot gun control stories into the limited space available, terrible anti-gun bills may be moving through Congress or your state legislature, and most gun-owners may have no idea that there is a danger.

In the newsletter (as elsewhere) be generous in praise for people who have helped with the group.

Legislators, being human (usually), like praise just as much as everyone else—more so, in fact, since they keep their jobs only as long as they stay popular. So use the newsletter to give full recognition to public officials who have voted for or otherwise helped the pro-rights cause. If the legislator gave a good speech on the floor of the legislator when she voted for the bill, reprint the speech in your newsletter.

While all legislators are hungry for praise, urban Congresspeople are especially hungry. In many states, including California, North Carolina, Florida, and New York, Congressional districts are twisted, bizarre oddities that run in thin strips from county to another to another, turn, and then veer off for the next county at a strange angle. These gerrymandered monstrosities mean that the Representative elected to the district does not represent a single town, or a cohesive group of neighborhoods, but instead represents disparate slices of several towns, or freakish slices of various neighborhoods. The result of all this is that the Congressman may have a hard time getting attention from the home-town newspaper, since he doesn't represent any full town. Consequently, the Congressman is all the hungrier for good publicity wherever he can find it—and your newsletter should supply it.

Awards

Besides giving pro-rights legislators good coverage in your newsletter, you may want to give an annual award to an outstanding legislator or two. The award can be announced at an annual dinner (if your group has one), or similar occasion. Or the award can simply be mailed to the legislator, along with a nice cover letter. An engraved wall plaque will be appreciated, especially by state and local officials. The inscription on the plaque could read something like this:

OUTSTANDING LEGISLATOR OF THE YEAR
presented to
State Representative
Walter E. Dilworthy
for his energetic and devoted
work in defense of
the Right to Keep and Bear Arms
March 22, 1990
Central Outerway Citizens for Safety

Leafleting and Information Tables

Places to hand out leaflets include any large public area, such as fairs, shopping malls, museums, government buildings, colleges, office buildings, factories, and especially college student unions. Door-to-door leafleting is also possible, but make sure that volunteers don't put leaflets into mail boxes. The United States Postal Service zealously guards its mail monopoly, and putting material without a stamp into a mailbox is a fast road to ruin. (We don't make the rules; we're just letting you know.)

Set up an information table at a shopping mall (ask permission first) or a public event such as a street fair. Posters, banners, and the like help draw attention to the table. Or just hand out literature there. When handing out literature, make sure to emphasize that it's free.

Shopping malls, like other places which are private property, have a right to exclude you, in most states. If the mall security officer tells you to stop leafleting, respect the mall owners' property rights.

Smiles are always important when meeting the public, but they're particularly helpful when leafleting.

Everything in a leaflet (like everything else you put in print) should be backed up with authoritative sources that you can document.

Information tables are good places to encourage letter-writing. Bring a list of the relevant addresses, and a healthy supply of stationary and pens. (See also chapter 17, on computer-generated letters.) Public areas are also good places to collect signatures on petitions.

If you can, bring a television and VCR, and keep pro-rights tapes playing.

And after you're done with the day's literature distribution, police the entire area to pick up any material of yours that might have been littered on the premises. Going out of your way to be a considerate guest raises your chances of being allowed to come back.

Information tables can also raise a little money by selling t-shirts, buttons, and the like. The NRA and the Citizens Committee for the Right to Keep and Bear Arms have a good supply of merchandise that they make available at wholesale prices to grassroots groups.

Media

One of your main objectives will be to get media coverage of your group's activities, so as to bring your message to many more people than you could through direct contacts.

Make a list of media contacts in your area, and keep it updated. The list should include not only media addresses, but also the names of the reporters and editorial writers who keep doing stories about gun issues. Since a media career requires frequently changes of assignment—and of employer—keep the list fresh.

Don't snub the small papers in your area (like the give-away weeklies). They're much easier to get coverage in than are large urban dailies.

Remember that the news media exist to cover news. Just articulating a position isn't newsworthy. Taking action (especially the kind of action that creates interesting photos) is newsworthy.

Anytime you're trying to get the local press to cover something, make sure it has a local angle. Even if the issue is a national rather than a local one, find a local angle on it. For example, while the Congressional debate on banning so-called "assault weapons" is a national issue, the fact that a local gun club is using them in a tournament is a local angle.

Never say anything to any journalist that you don't want to see in print. Many journalists will keep a promise of confidentiality, or of being "off-the-record," but some don't.

Strive to make yourself useful to the local media. Provide them with useful, accurate information. Everything the media ask from you, they will ask on short notice, because the reporters themselves are under time deadlines. Help the reporters out by being able to fit with their schedules, by suggesting additional sources for them to interview, and by remembering that while the media as a whole may be biased, every individual reporter should be treated with respect.

Once your quotes start appearing in print and broadcast reports, your influence will be magnified. Not only will you be reaching larger audiences, elected officials will begin to see the media take your group seriously, and may start to do the same themselves.

Finances

As the above sections on fundraising ideas have indicated, money will always be tight. At the same time, the group's finances may be closely watched by government regulators. So keep close track of your finances, right from the start.

Believe it or not, while you'll be poor, many folks will think that you're rich, because they've fallen for the myth that "the gun lobby" is made out of cash.

Elections

Chapter 23 contains detailed advice for how to participate in elections effectively.

Finally, don't be afraid to ask for help. The Citizens Committee for the Right to Keep and Bear Arms would be glad to offer you advice on anything you need. And your NRA State Liaison—while usually very busy—will also be eager to help grassroots organizations. The NRA also has staff assigned fulltime to assisting grassroots groups. Your local bookstore's or library's business section will have several advice books on how to run a non-profit association.

31. How to Write a News Release

"IF YE LOVE WEALTH MORE THAN LIBERTY, THE
TRANQUILLITY OF SERVITUDE GREATER THAN THE
ANIMATING CONTEST FOR FREEDOM, GO HOME AND
LEAVE US IN PEACE. WE SEEK NOT YOUR COUNCIL,
NOR YOUR ARMS. CROUCH DOWN AND LICK THE
HAND THAT FEEDS YOU; AND MAY POSTERITY FORGET
THAT YE WERE OUR COUNTRY MEN."

—Samuel Adams

Timing

Send the news release out well in advance of the event
you want covered. Many small newspapers publish only once a
week, so get the release to them in plenty of time for their own
deadlines. If you have any doubts about timing, call their office,
and ask about their deadlines. As a rule of thumb, try to send the
release at least 15 days in advance of the event.

If you know of a particular person at the media outlet
who might be interested in doing a story based on your event,
send the release addressed to them. (And to be safe, send another
copy of the release just addressed to the media outlet.)

On the morning of the event, call the places you've
already sent the press release to, and remind them about the
event. Send a fax of the press release too.

Style

A press release should never be more than 2 pages long
(one page is better), and should be double-spaced, with wide
margins.

Since the media receive literally dozens of press releases a day, do what you can with graphics to make it look
attractive. Put an interesting title on top. If your organization has
a logo, use it. And print the release on colored paper. (This last
suggestion applies to releases that will be mailed or hand-
delivered, and not to faxed releases.) When choosing colors,
avoid red, since red is an "emotional" color, and the whole

object of the pro-rights effort is to help undecided folks look at the issue in a rational, non-hysterical manner.

There should be at least a one-inch margin at the left, right, top, and bottom of the page. (This applies to any kind of written output, in fact.)

Proofread the draft release numerous times, and verify every fact contained in the release.

Ideally, the entire text of the press release should not occupy more than one side of a sheet of paper. If the press release absolutely requires more than one page, put your group's name, the title of the press release, and the name and phone number of the contact person at the top of the second page.

Press releases sent to the print media should be written so that they are ready to insert in the publication, as a self-standing story. Likewise, press releases for the radio should be capable of being read on the air.

Proofread it again, just before you send it out.

Substance

When print or radio editors need to cut a story for length, they generally cut from the bottom. So make sure that all the most essential information is at the beginning, not the end. Press releases should use the "inverted pyramid" writing style, whereby the most important facts come first, the less important facts in the middle, and the least important facts at the end. Saving the best material for the end is all right for detective novels, but not for press releases.

The opening sentence of the press release must have a strong lead that grabs the reader's attention. The second paragraph of the news release can be used to explain the significance of the event. By the end of the first two paragraphs, you should have supplied all of the "five Ws" (who, what, where, when, and why. And also how).

In addition, show the "human interest" aspect to your release, emphasizing who your story affects, and how it affects them. For example:

For immediate release

For more information, contact:
Bob Skjellyfeti (505) 555-8740.

Gun Safety Classes

> *Firearms safety classes for the community will be held on June 18, at the North Shore Gun Club. The four-hour classes are free to the public, and begin at 1 p.m at the 509 West Main Street.*
> *Club President Jackie Jackson explained that the recent surge in gun ownership after the Los Angeles riots makes it especially important that gun owners learn proper safety techniques. Ms. Jackson added that everyone in the community is welcome to attend, whether or not they own a gun. Persons without their own gun may borrow a club gun to use at the range.*

The last paragraph can include a brief description of the group sending the press release. Make sure that the release includes the name, address, phone number, and contact person for the group.

Content

Press releases should not be sent out as a writing exercise. Send them only when there is something genuinely newsworthy. The subject must have immediacy (be about something that's happening now, or will happen soon), and must have a local angle to it. Ideally, the subject should relate to some other event currently in the news.

The press release should be written so as to stimulate a reporter's interest in covering the story himself, and to provide the person who compiles the newspaper's "community calendar" section with concise information to insert a paragraph about your event.

32. Public Service Announcements

Public service announcements are free advertising, run by the media as a public service. They most commonly appear on radio, sometimes on television, and once in a while in print media.

Because radio and television broadcast licenses are allocated by the Federal Communication Commission "in the public interest" (theoretically), stations like to broadcast public service announcements to show how public-minded they are. PSAs also help fill up unsold advertising slots.

Radio

Let's start with radio. Every radio station will have someone in charge of PSAs. Call your local stations, learn who the PSA person is, and find out what the station's PSA guidelines are. All future communications with the station should be aimed at the PSA person.

The PSA for the radio station will be a neatly-typed script that a station DJ/announcer can read on the air. The script should be about 20 seconds (40-50 words) long, unless station guidelines specify a different length.

Read the PSA out loud to yourself many times, so that you can revise it and make it as close to perfect as you can get.

The PSA should conclude with a tag line indicating who produced the PSA, such as "This announcement brought to you by the North Eastwick Rifle Club."

Also on the PSA sheet (but not in the on-the-air script) should be a contact person and a telephone number, so that the station can contact you if there are questions.

Public service announcements have to relate to some type of public service. Political and/or legislative material is not allowed. Nor should any person or organization be criticized.

The PSA should involve something to do with community programs or education, rather than with anything partisan or for-profit. Examples of PSAs could include: announcing an upcoming safety class at a local gun club; informing the public about an upcoming speech or debate; urging people who have firearms to store them safely; or telling children that if they find a gun, they should not touch it, should leave the area immediately, and should tell an adult.

Once you've got a good PSA written, send copies to all radio stations in your area that do PSAs.

The NRA can also help you with PSAs, especially for the group's Eddie Eagle child safety program.

Television

The same general guidelines used for radio apply to television. While most radio PSAs will be broadcast late at night (when it's harder for the station to sell advertising slots), virtually every television PSA will be late-nighter. (That means 2 a.m., not during the Tonight Show.)

While a radio PSA can simply be a written script, you'll have to give the television station a ready-to-use videotape. That's not as hard as it might sound. If you live in an area with cable TV, there will be at least one "public access" channel. The purpose of the public access channel is to help ordinary folks produce and air TV shows. So if you make an appointment for studio time at the public access station, the staff will be glad to help you produce a short commercial for use as a PSA. (Of course you'll have to think up all the content; the staff can only help with production.)

If you absolutely can't create a videotape, at least supply the station with a few high-quality slides.

Print Media

Broadcast media was invented at about the same time as the federal government's explosive growth in the 1920s and 1930s. Print media, in contrast, is older than America. As a result, print media grew to maturity long before government could get ahold of it, and print media is subject to much less regulation than broadcast media. Newspapers, unlike radio and television stations, don't need government licenses, and don't have government officials reviewing their content (usually).

The greater independence of print media is good in general, but bad for PSAs, since the print media don't have to convince any FCC official that the media are acting "in the public interest."

And while radio and television stations can't stop broadcasting simply because they have empty advertising slots, a newspaper or magazine that doesn't sell enough advertising simply prints fewer pages. As a result, the print media has much less incentive than the broadcast media to run PSAs.

Nevertheless, PSAs do find their way into print media. First of all, press releases which get printed sometimes function as a kind of PSA.

Secondly, some print media (particularly the smaller, newer ones) will run free advertising for public interest groups that the publisher likes. For example, the advertising space you see for the "Partnership for a Drug-Free America" is donated by the host newspaper or magazine. (Much of the Partnership advertising is, unfortunately, just as hysterical and factually incorrect as advertising from the anti-gun lobby.)

If you have a friendship with a local publisher, ask her if she would be interested in running some pro-rights advertising as a public service. The Second Amendment Foundation, CCRKBA, and the NRA all have camera-ready copy (meaning that the advertisement needs no layout or other further production work) which they can send to any interested newspaper or magazine.

33. SUPPORT OTHER PRO-RIGHTS ORGANIZATIONS

"ETHICAL INSIGHTS ARE BORN IN ATTACKS UPON CONFORMITY TO EXISTING MORES." —Rollo May.

One of the greatest strengths of the anti-gun lobbies is their ability to network with like-minded organizations and leaders. The Coalition to Stop Gun Violence (formerly the National Coalition to Ban Handguns) has relatively few actual members. But the Coalition networks with powerful organizations whose leaders support gun prohibition, and thereby achieves far more influence than it could solely on the strength of its membership base.

Likewise, Handgun Control, Inc. does an outstanding job at reaching out to important political and other leaders to enlist them in the cause. While these leaders are usually not interested enough in the gun issue to play a major role (otherwise they would already have volunteered to help HCI), they are happy to add their name to a press release, or put in a good word with a Congressperson they know, if HCI comes to them, and makes it easy for them to help.

Just as the anti-gun lobby has increased its clout by copying many of the tactical innovations of the pro-rights lobby (such as effective use of direct mail), pro-rights folks should take a leaf from the opposition, and work to build bridges with sympathetic community leaders.

For instance, suppose you're friends with a physician. Also suppose that your state legislature is considering whether to require that licensed, trained citizens be allowed to carry concealed handguns for protection. At an appropriate moment, ask her what she thinks of the gun issue. If she says "I think people ought to be able to have guns for protection, but I don't see why the NRA is so crazy that it won't even accept a waiting period."

At this point you do not engage her in a debate over waiting periods. Instead, you express your agreement with her basic attitude about guns. Then bring up the concealed carry bill in the legislature, and see what she thinks of it—especially in light of the fact that licenses would only be issued after there is a background check, and proof of safety training.

If she likes the general idea, suggest that her support might help the carry reform bill get enacted. Perhaps she could testify before a legislative committee, and explain why doctors—who must sometimes carry controlled prescription drugs while traveling—are robbery targets, and need guns for protection. Or maybe she would just want to write a letter to her State Senator. If she says she'd like to help, you could offer to draft a letter for her consideration.

There's no limit to the kinds of folks who can approached for assistance: religious leaders, union officials, professional associations, teachers, professors, scientists, and more. Some will rebuff you; others will be delighted to be asked and will be willing to do something major (such as give a speech to a local group like the Rotary); some will do something smaller, like write to their Congressperson; and others may just ask you to send them more information.

Prior to a meeting with anyone you don't know well, it always helps to learn a little bit about what makes them tick. As detailed in chapter 22 (finding out more about your legislators), computer databases such as Prodigy, Compuserve, and Nexis; and the *Martindale Hubbell* legal directory can provide you with some basic background about community leaders. Public libraries contain numerous other biographical guides which you may find helpful.

Making alliances with local activist groups involved in other issues is often an effective tactic. One obstacle to such alliances is that each group wants to stick to its own agenda, for fear of alienating members on peripheral issues. For example, your local gun group probably wouldn't want to take a stand on abortion, since the gun group probably includes members who are pro-choice and other members who are pro-life. Likewise the local tax limitation group may feel uncomfortable taking a stand on gun control. But there is a way to finesse this problem: each group can pick an angle to the issue that fits within the group's own agenda. For example, your gun group and the local anti-tax group might agree that they both oppose a proposed increase in gun licensing fees.

The more you can get other groups involved, even if peripherally, in the gun issue, the more impressed elected officials will be about the importance of gun rights. For instance, the anti-tax group might send legislators a 20-item questionnaire to determine election-year endorsements. If one of the questions is "Do you support or oppose Governor Baldbreath's proposal to double the fee for gun licenses?" the legislator reading the questionnaire will start to get the idea that gun freedom is important to more than just gun organizations.

And if an organization just flat-out turns you down, don't walk away in a huff. Accept their decision, but ask if you can send them information about the issue from time to time. Over the long run, patient outreach can make quite a change. In the early 1960s, the Sierra Club favored nuclear power, and Planned Parenthood opposed abortion. Over time, dedicated activists convinced those groups to change their mind.

34. Parting Shots

"THE LIBERTIES OF OUR COUNTRY, THE FREEDOM OF OUR CIVIL CONSTITUTION, ARE WORTH DEFENDING AT ALL HAZARDS; AND IT IS OUR DUTY TO DEFEND THEM AGAINST ALL ATTACKS. WE HAVE RECEIVED THEM AS A FAIR INHERITANCE FROM OUR WORTHY ANCESTORS: THEY PURCHASED THEM FOR US WITH TOIL AND DANGER AND EXPENSE OF TREASURE AND BLOOD, AND TRANSMITTED TO US WITH CARE AND DILIGENCE. IT WILL BRING AN EVERLASTING MARK OF INFAMY ON THE PRESENT GENERATION, ENLIGHTENED AS IT IS, IF WE SHOULD SUFFER THEM TO BE WRESTED FROM US BY VIOLENCE WITHOUT A STRUGGLE, OR BE CHEATED OUT OF THEM BY THE ARTIFICES OF FALSE AND DESIGNING MEN." —Samuel Adams, 1771.

Like Hollywood, we believe that anything that's worth doing right is worth a sequel. So we're already at work on volume two of this book, which will cover material that we couldn't fit in the first book. We'll go into topics such as which corporations support or oppose the Second Amendment, how gun clubs and gun stores can maximize their effectiveness in supporting civil liberties, which gun companies really support the right to bear arms, and how you can fight back against media bias. Plus plenty of other topics.

If you have suggestions about what has worked for you—regarding any type of pro-rights activism—drop us a line, and maybe we'll be able to include your advice in Volume 2. Send your note to: Alan Gottlieb & Dave Kopel, Volume 2 Project, Citizens Committee for the Right to Keep and Bear Arms, 12500 NE Tenth Place, Bellevue, WA 98005.

NOTES

NOTES

NOTES

QUANTITY DISCOUNTS
Things You Can Do To Defend Your Gun Rights
Give a copy to everyone you know!

Now is the time to get this book into the hands of every American. Order 25, 50 or 100 copies. Send them to your friends. Give them to business associates. Mail one to everyone you know.

DISCOUNT SCHEDULE

1 copy	$9.95	25 copies	$175.00
5 copies	$45.00	50 copies	$300.00
10 copies	$85.00	100 copies	$500.00
	500 copies	$2,000.00	

ORDER YOURS TODAY!

Merril Press
P.O. Box 1682
Bellevue, WA 98009

Please send me _____ copies of THINGS YOU CAN DO TO DEFEND YOUR GUN RIGHTS. Enclosed is a check or money order for $_____.

Please charge my ☐ VISA ☐ MasterCard
Number_____Expires_____
Signature_____
Print Name_____
Street_____
City_____
State_____ZIP_____
Phone (_____)_____

QUANTITY DISCOUNTS
Things You Can Do To Defend Your Gun Rights
Give a copy to everyone you know!

Now is the time to get this book into the hands of every American. Order 25, 50 or 100 copies. Send them to your friends. Give them to business associates. Mail one to everyone you know.

DISCOUNT SCHEDULE

1 copy	$9.95	25 copies	$175.00
5 copies	$45.00	50 copies	$300.00
10 copies	$85.00	100 copies	$500.00
	500 copies	$2,000.00	

ORDER YOURS TODAY!

Merril Press
P.O. Box 1682
Bellevue, WA 98009

Please send me _____ copies of THINGS YOU CAN DO TO DEFEND YOUR GUN RIGHTS. Enclosed is a check or money order for $_____.

Please charge my ☐ VISA ☐ MasterCard

Number_____Expires_____

Signature_____

Print Name_____

Street_____

City_____

State_____ZIP_____

Phone (_____)_____